Flavors of Hungary

Flavors of Hungary

By Charlotte Slovak Biro

Drawings by Linda Robertson

101 Productions

San Francisco

1973

Fifth Printing, May 1981

Distributed to the Book Trade in the United States of America
by Charles Scribner's Sons, New York

Library of Congress Catalog Card Number 73-81085

PUBLISHED BY 101 PRODUCTIONS
834 Mission Street
San Francisco, California 94103

Contents

With all my love to my daughters
Agi and Panni
and in the nicest memory of my
Mother and Father
who loved so dearly the good Earth.

Introduction

If my childhood had not been so perfectly wonderful, with the warmest family ties, I wouldn't have been able to survive the more difficult chapters of my life to come.

As the youngest in my family, with two older brothers, I was very pampered; although when it came to fatherly discipline, I was the one who received punishment from the temperamental patriarch instead of my brothers. Due to my mother's frail health, I took over the care of the family and maids, managing the household at a very early age.

As every well-bred, young person, I received a wonderful education in languages. German, French and English were equally important. I was very fond of music and studied piano from a concert artist—a sweet, grey-haired lady who predicted a great future for me as a pianist. She never would have guessed that my talents would be used to coach my grandchildren.

Skating and dancing were our favorite pastimes. We danced both classical Dalcrose barefoot in black, satin, Greek skirts and ballroom dancing in long, formal Biedermeyer gowns. In spring and summer we played tennis and went swimming.

Thus, I was well-equipped physically and emotionally for the storms that life later brought to me.

When I was married, my generous parents provided me with an elegant home on the Danube-quay. My dowry included a big, valuable vineyard in Badacsony by Lake Balaton. I later received another vineyard so that I would be able to give each of my daughters one of the estates when they were grown.

Life was beautiful, both socially and financially. My husband was in a high position in the Credit Bank. Our household was well run and included maids and a German governess. Summer was spent in the vineyard with many guests; in winter music and entertainment were shared with friends in Budapest.

The vineyards gave not only a large income but a full pantry. We had our own harvested flour, fruits and vegetables. The butcher prepared our ham, bacon and sausage. Chickens, ducks, geese raised from eggs, wine, and brandy were all available in large quantities.

My father saved the best wine from the years my two daughters were born for their wedding

Introduction

days. When we last tasted a drop of the wine, it looked like gold and tasted of the best nectar. Our lives were to change, however, and my daughters were never to taste of the wine. And what became of the gorgeous life? War and revolution!

The Germans took away everything; they destroyed our home by bombing, and completely emptied our vineyards. We spent much of our time in a bomb shelter, burning oil for light. With our big reserve of food, we were better off than others for a time. However, we soon came to know what starvation meant. We ate snow to replace water, and what I baked from dried peas became a pancake-like patty cooked on a chestnut oven. (I can promise that I haven't included this recipe in this book.)

When the war was over, we established a new home and invested in the vineyards to start a new life, but nothing was the same. We couldn't forget the explosions of the bombs or our fear; in our minds and in our hearts, we couldn't find peace and a faith in the future. Hungary became a communist state, and property was nationalized.

Few people found happiness during this time. They whispered among themselves of the changes in their country and of their unhappiness. One wish kept us alive—to leave our old country, to find freedom somewhere else. At night we listened to news on the radio of illegal border crossings. By day my daughters pleaded with me to leave Hungary. This was the most difficult time of my life and the hardest decision I've ever made—to stay or to leave. It took months to shape up a plan.

We finally found people who knew where we could cross the border at night through the mined barbed wire. Our two daughters went across first. (We did not want to give up our home until we knew they were safe.) I still shake when I remember their night departure. The next day the message came that they had arrived safely in Vienna. My husband and I then proceeded to cross the border in the same way. Our try was not so successful. We were caught and put in prison.

I didn't want to believe that instead of embracing my daughters, I was locked in a cell. It was winter and bitter cold; we slept on a thin layer of old straw and were constantly awakened at night for interrogation. When we were questioned, they examined my small bundle and found my recipe book and apron. For me this meant luck, since I was able to work in the kitchen, which had a wood-burning stove, and to be near food. The guards were served first; the prisoners ate the leftovers. I can remember the first time I ate from a bended metal plate with a cracked spoon. I didn't need salt, as my tears were floating in the soup.

The prisoners were all political except for the cook. He was a real convict, a murderer. I was assigned to help him with the cooking. When he fixed rice the whole kitchen was like a skating rink, as he poured the starchy water from the big kettle onto the floor.

I could write pages about my experiences that winter, but I try to overcome thoughts of the cold cells, the snow up to our knees, and the rattling of chains. The saddest part was that I was separated from my dearest ones. It was eight long years before we were reunited. My husband was never to see his children again, as he died soon after we were released from prison.

When the big revolution came in 1956, officials began to let older people leave the country, as there was a great shortage of housing. After much red tape I "traded" my apartment for a passport.

My children had grown into adults. They had been taken to the United States by my brother—the pioneer in the family. Thanks to his patronage each of my daughters had a college diploma and a fine home. They also had good, American husbands. After my release, I came to the United States and tried my best to adjust to a new world, but it is a long way from the Danube to the Pacific.

Throughout my 17 years in America, I have often entertained my children's American friends. I always surprise them with something from Hungary. After the meal, the guests always want my recipes. For this reason, I decided to share my traditional family recipes. My basic concern is not to waste any part of the food. For having owned abundant estates, I knew how to manage well. For having experienced poverty, I learned the importance of economy. There is a saying that "you can save only when you have."

My old, shattered, hand-written recipe book, which even accompanied me to prison, was started by my mother; both my husband and my children had their favorite recipes. It has been used so much that it is ready to fall apart.

Hungary's history has had an effect on its cuisine. The Austro-Hungarian Empire with all its nationalities shows the greatest influence. The Wiener schnitzel, sauerkraut, sauerbraten, dumplings, and Sacher torte are all part of the Austrian heritage and are as popular as the local specialties.

In spite of foreign influence, our food has retained its originality. It is limitlessly tasty with an imagination that is uniquely its own, blending the flavors of east and west. Paprika gives the national character to Hungarian food, and adds charm with its "sweet and noble" *(edes nemes)* flavor. It should be noted that when I list paprika as an ingredient in my recipes, I am referring to Hungarian rose paprika.

Hungarian cooking uses very few spices; the main idea is to bring out the natural flavors of the ingredients through special cooking techniques. The gravy, for example, is especially important in Hungarian dishes. Onion is often browned slowly in bacon drippings or fat, giving the gravy a better aroma, flavor, and color. This is only one characteristic of Hungarian culinary style; others will be mentioned throughout the book.

Once you have tried some of these recipes, you will find Hungarian food is easy to prepare. The recipes in this book are meant for four to six persons, so eat with a hearty appetite.

Jo etvagyat!

Charlotte Biro
August, 1973

Soups and Garnishes

Soups play an important role in the eating habits of Hungarians. When meat, fish, or poultry are added, they may be served as the main course. Making a good soup requires care and time so that all the flavors can be drawn from the meat and bones.

The variety of soups is as limitless as the cook's imagination. The most well-known soup in Hungary is goulash *(gulyas)* which originated when the Magyar (Hungarians) were still nomadic tribes. It was cooked over an open fire in smoky kettles. Through the years, the popularity of goulash has been one of the most famous contributions of Hungary to international cuisine.

At the end of this chapter, I have included recipes for the garnishes traditionally served with soup.

Soups and Garnishes

GOULASH
(Gulyas)

4 slices bacon
2 medium-sized onions, sliced
1 to 1-1/2 tablespoons Hungarian paprika
2 pounds chuck, blade, or boneless
   pot roast, cut into small cubes
1 tablespoon salt
1 teaspoon caraway seeds
1 green pepper, sliced
1 tomato, sliced
2 cloves garlic, finely minced
4 small potatoes, pared and quartered
pinched noodles (see page 23)
green pepper rings for garnish

Brown bacon in a Dutch oven or heavy, 3-quart pot with a tight-fitting lid. Remove bacon and brown onions in the bacon drippings until transparent.

Remove pot from heat and stir in paprika. Add the beef, salt, caraway seeds, cooked bacon, and half of the green pepper and tomato.

Return to heat and cover tightly. Simmer over low heat, stirring occasionally and adding small amounts of water as needed. Cook 1-1/2 to 2 hours or until meat is tender.

Add garlic, potatoes, the other half of the green pepper and the tomato. Add enough water to completely cover the meat and vegetables. Bring to a boil and simmer for 30 minutes. In the last 10 minutes add the pinched noodles.

Serve hot in individual soup bowls or from a soup tureen. Garnish with green pepper rings.

Serves 4 to 6

Variation: Lamb Goulash

Lamb goulash is made following the same method as beef goulash. However, less bacon drippings are needed as lamb has more fatty tissues. Also, more green pepper and paprika are added. Lamb goulash is excellent highly spiced and gives the diner an excuse to wash it down with a vintage wine. This brings back memories of our vineyards.

Lamb goulash was traditionally served to the harvesters at our vineyard in Badacsony. The rich flavor of the lamb goes well with the hot, mulled wine served during the harvesting. The harvest was often delayed until the late fall in favor of a better quality wine. The riper the grape, the more sugar content and the higher the volume of alcohol. Once harvesting began, the men worked in day and night shifts—the pickers during the day and the pressmen both day and night. The caretakers and servants had hot lamb goulash prepared at midnight to serve the workers. We had our own lamb flocks to serve this need, and day after day we looked forward to the goulash and the mulled wine. We never grew tired of it.

CHICKEN BROTH
(Ujhazi Tyukleves)

2 pounds whole chicken, or
   2-1/2 pounds chicken backs
8 cups cold water
3 to 4 carrots
2 to 3 stalks celery
1/2 green pepper
1 small tomato
2 to 3 green onions
1-1/2 teaspoons salt
8 to 10 peppercorns
4 to 5 sprigs parsley
1 celery root, peeled and sliced (optional)
1/4 pound green peas (optional)
1/4 pound mushrooms (optional)
2 small potatoes, peeled (optional)
liver dumplings (see page 23) or
   noodles (see page 23) for garnish

Put the chicken in a large pot and cover with cold water. Bring to a boil, reduce heat, and simmer 1 hour. Add remaining ingredients and cook for another hour. Celery root, green peas, mushrooms, and potatoes may also be added, as they contribute to the delicate flavor of the broth.

When chicken and vegetables are tender, strain and defat 3/4 of the broth and keep meat and vegetables hot in the remaining broth until ready to serve. Cook dumplings in the strained broth. If a whole chicken has been used in making the soup, it can be served with a mushroom or tomato sauce. Arrange the chicken on a platter surrounded by the cooked vegetables. Serve the sauce on the side. Serve the clear broth garnished with liver dumplings or noodles.

Or if desired, the vegetables and deboned chicken may be cut up and added to the broth.

Serves 6

Chicken salad: If the soup has been made from chicken backs, the chicken may be cut up, along with some of the vegetables, to make chicken salad. Add some sliced pickles, 1 to 2 hard-boiled eggs, and mayonnaise. Serve on lettuce leaves.

Chicken aspic: Debone and cut up chicken, along with some of the vegetables. Return to the broth. To every 2 cups of broth, add 1 envelope unflavored gelatin. Dissolve gelatin in a cup of the broth; mix with remaining broth. Put in a ring mold well brushed with oil and chill until firm.

Soups and Garnishes

BEEF BROTH
(Husleves)

1-1/2 pounds lean beef
2 to 3 beef soup bones
8 cups cold water
1 tablespoon salt
8 peppercorns
1 large onion
2 cloves garlic
4 carrots, cut in half
4 stalks celery, cut in half
5 sprigs parsley
2 cabbage leaves
1 small tomato
1 green pepper
cream of wheat dumplings (see page 24)
    for garnish

Combine the beef, soup bones, water, salt, and peppercorns in a large pot with a tight-fitting lid. Bring to a boil, reduce heat, and simmer 30 minutes. Skim off foam.

Add the onion, garlic, carrots, celery, parsley, cabbage leaves, tomato, and green pepper. If necessary, add more water. Cover tightly and simmer 2 hours or until meat is tender.

Strain 3/4 of the broth. Keep the meat and vegetables hot in the remaining broth until ready to serve. When serving, arrange on large platter. Serve with the broth to which precooked dumplings have been added.

Serves 6

HANGOVER SOUP
(Korhelyleves)

3 slices bacon
1 small onion, chopped
1 teaspoon Hungarian paprika
4 cups water
1 to 2 ham hocks
1 green pepper, sliced
1 tomato
1 16-ounce can sauerkraut, washed
1 tablespoon all-purpose flour
1/2 pint sour cream
1/2 pound Polish sausage

Brown bacon in a Dutch oven or heavy, 3-quart pot with a tight-fitting lid. Remove bacon and brown onions in the bacon drippings until transparent.

Add paprika, water, ham hocks, green pepper, and tomatoes to the pot. Simmer 1-1/2 hours or until meat is tender.

Add the sauerkraut and cook for 20 minutes (be careful not to overcook).

Combine flour and sour cream and add to the soup mixture, along with the sausage. If ham hocks have been used, debone and return meat to the soup. Bring soup to a boil and serve hot with additional sour cream on the side.

Serves 4 to 6

This soup is named after the famous Hungarian actor, Ujhazi. It was his favorite.

One of the most famous coffee houses in Budapest—called "New York"—specializes in catering to the after-theatre crowd. From midnight until morning, they serve hangover soup, chicken broth, and pork and beans. The elegant setting of the restaurant is the meeting place for all the prominent people in art, music, literature, and the theatre.

Soups and Garnishes

PORK AND BEANS
(Bableves)

4 slices bacon
1 large onion, sliced
1 tablespoon Hungarian paprika
1 pound red beans, uncooked
1 small tomato, sliced
1 green pepper, sliced
2 ham hocks, or 1 pound picnic ham
2 to 3 cloves garlic, finely minced
8 cups water
1/2 pound Polish sausage

Brown bacon in a Dutch oven or heavy, 3-quart pot with a tight-fitting lid. Remove bacon and brown onions in the bacon drippings until transparent.

Add paprika, beans, tomato, green pepper, ham hocks, bacon, garlic, and water. Simmer 1-1/2 hours or until meat is tender, stirring occasionally and adding small amounts of water as needed. (Vary the amount of water according to whether a soup or a stew consistency is desired.)

Add sausage during the last 10 minutes of cooking. If ham hocks have been used, debone and return meat to the soup.

Pork and beans are good prepared a day ahead and reheated at 300° for 1 hour.

Serves 6

SOUR EGG SOUP
(Hot or Jellied)
(Savanyutojas)

2 tablespoons all-purpose flour
3 tablespoons butter, melted
5 cups water
1 teaspoon salt
1 tablespoon white vinegar
2 bay leaves
2 green onions
6 eggs
1/2 cup sour cream
sugar as desired

Hot: Brown flour in melted butter until golden. Add water and stir until smooth. Add salt, vinegar, bay leaves, and green onions. Simmer 10 minutes. Break in eggs, one by one, and cook until egg whites turn color and yolks are still soft inside. If desired, put a little sugar in the soup. Add sour cream just before serving; do not bring to a boil.

Jellied: Prepare a ring mold or small, individual molds by brushing with oil. Combine water, salt, vinegar, bay leaves, green onions, sugar, and 1/4 cup raisins. Break in eggs, one by one, and cook until egg whites turn color. Discard green onion. To every 2 cups of soup, add 1 envelope unflavored gelatin. Dissolve gelatin in a cup of the soup; mix with remaining soup. Arrange eggs in molds and pour soup over. Chill until firm.

Serves 4 to 6

VEGETABLE SOUPS
(Zoldseg Leves)

4 to 6 veal bones, or leftover bones from chicken
1 teaspoon salt
2 to 3 green onions
1 clove garlic
5 to 6 peppercorns
8 cups water
2 carrots, 2 stalks celery, 1 parsnip
butter dumplings (see page 24) for garnish

Combine all ingredients in a large pot and simmer slowly for 2 hours. Strain twice to make a clear stock.

Cauliflower, potatoes, asparagus, or fresh green peas can be added to the stock, along with parsley. Simmer 30 minutes; add dumplings.

Creamed soups: Purée vegetable soup in a blender. Return to heat and simmer gently for 10 minutes. Combine 1/2 cup sour cream or heavy, sweet cream and 2 to 3 tablespoons flour. Mix into soup and simmer until warm; do not boil. Garnish with croutons.

Serves 6

RAGOUT SOUP
(Raguleves)

giblets of 2 chickens, or
   2 or 3 pieces of veal knuckle
3 tablespoons butter, melted
1/2 green pepper, cut up
1 small tomato, cut up
2 carrots, sliced
2 stalks celery, sliced
1/2 onion, finely minced
1 tablespoon all-purpose flour
2 tablespoons minced parsley
5 cups water, or chicken broth
1 teaspoon salt
5 or 6 mushrooms, sliced
butter dumplings (see page 24) for garnish

Sauté cut up giblets and vegetables in melted butter. When golden brown, add onion and brown until transparent.

Add flour to onions and stir. Add parsley, water, and salt. Simmer gently for 1 hour or until meat is tender.

Add mushrooms and butter dumplings the last 10 minutes of cooking.

If ragout soup is made from veal knuckles, cook bones in water until meat is tender. Debone and use meat in place of chicken giblets. Veal stock can replace water.

Serves 4

CREAMED POTATO SOUP
(*Tejfeles Krumplileves*)

3 to 4 potatoes
8 cups beef broth, or 8 cups water flavored
   with 3 bouillon cubes
1/2 onion, minced
2 to 3 stalks celery, minced
1/2 green pepper, minced
parsley to taste
1 teaspoon salt
3 tablespoons butter
2 tablespoons all-purpose flour
1/2 pint sour cream, or heavy cream
1 to 2 egg yolks
parsley and chives, finely chopped, for garnish
croutons (see page 22) or golden drops
   (see page 25) for garnish

Peel and cut potatoes in large pieces. Add to broth along with onion, celery, green pepper, parsley, and salt. Simmer 45 minutes or until vegetables are tender. When tender, put soup through a sieve or purée in a blender.

Melt butter in a saucepan. Add flour and brown, stirring constantly 2 to 3 minutes. Add to potato mixture and simmer 20 minutes. Add more salt if needed.

Put cream and egg yolks in soup tureen. Pour hot soup over and stir vigorously. Garnish with parsley and chives. Serve with croutons or golden drops on the side. May be served hot or cold.

Serves 6

POTATO SOUP, PEASANT STYLE
(*Paraszt Krumpli Leves*)

3 to 4 medium-sized potatoes
3 tablespoons butter or bacon drippings
2 tablespoons all-purpose flour
1 teaspoon Hungarian paprika
1 to 2 carrots
1/2 onion
1/2 small tomato, minced
1/2 small green pepper, minced
salt to taste
8 cups water

Peel and cut potatoes into small cubes. Reserve in cold water.

Melt butter or bacon drippings in a large pot with a tight-fitting lid. Add flour and stir constantly until golden brown.

Add paprika, potatoes, carrots, onion, tomato, green pepper, and salt. Pour water over to cover. Simmer covered until vegetables are tender. In Hungary, the juice of cooked celery root is often used in place of water. This enhances the flavor. The celery root can then be used to make celery root salad (see page 45).

For a simple meal, cook hot dogs and butter dumplings (see page 24) in the soup.

Serves 6

Soups and Garnishes

COLD GREEN BEAN SOUP
(Zoldbab Leves)

1 pound green beans
5 cups hot water
2 tablespoons finely chopped green onions
2 teaspoons salt
2 tablespoons sugar
1/2 pint sour cream
2 tablespoons all-purpose flour
3 tablespoons white vinegar

Cut the green beans into 1/2-inch pieces and put in a large pot with the water, onion, salt, and sugar. Simmer covered 20 minutes or until beans are tender.

Combine sour cream, flour, and 1/2 cup of the soup. Add to the remaining soup. Simmer 5 minutes. Add vinegar. Sweeten soup to taste. Cool and chill. Serve with extra sour cream.

Serves 4

CARAWAY SEED SOUP
(Komenymagos Leves)

1/3 cup butter
1/3 cup all-purpose flour
1 tablespoon caraway seeds
6 cups water
1-1/2 tablespoons salt
croutons (see page 22) for garnish

Melt butter in a large pot with a tight-fitting lid. Add flour and stir. Add caraway seeds, stirring constantly until golden brown. Remove from heat.

Gradually add water and salt, stirring constantly. Return to heat and bring to a boil, continuing to stir. Cover and simmer 15 minutes. Pour through a sieve. Garnish with croutons.

Variation: Creamed Caraway Seed Soup Just before serving, mix in 3/4 cup heavy cream.

Variation: Caraway Seed Soup with Eggs Add 2 well-beaten eggs. Stir with a whisk, beating eggs into lacy shreds.

Hungarians believe that caraway seed soup is the best remedy for an upset stomach. Some also believe it helps to increase the flow of milk in nursing mothers. The Romans chewed caraway seeds to mask bad breath, especially that resulting from overdrink.

COLD APPLE SOUP
(Hideg Alma Leves)

3 cups hot water
4 apples, pared and diced
1/2 cup sugar
1 lemon rind, finely chopped
juice of 1 lemon
2 tablespoons cold water
2 tablespoons all-purpose flour
1 cup white wine
1/2 cup heavy cream

Combine water, apples, sugar, lemon rind, and lemon juice. Cook until apples are tender. Blend cold water and flour and add to soup. Simmer 5 minutes. Stir in wine and sweeten soup to taste. Chill well covered and add cream before serving.

This is a basic recipe for all fruit soups. If fruit is already tart, do not use lemon juice. If fruit is seedy, put through a strainer.

Serves 4

COLD CHERRY SOUP
(Cseresnye Leves) Hiddegg megg levesh

48 32
2 16-ounce cans sour, pitted cherries
4,5 3 cups hot water
1.5 1 cup or more sugar
cinnamon to taste quté
3 2 tablespoons all-purpose flour
1 cup heavy cream 1/2 e
1 cup red wine or sherry

Combine cherries, water, sugar, and cinnamon in a large pot. Bring to a boil.

Meanwhile, mix flour and heavy cream until well blended; slowly pour into cherry mixture, stirring constantly. Bring to a boil and cook 3 to 5 minutes, stirring occasionally. Remove from heat.

Stir in wine or sherry. Sweeten soup to taste and chill well covered.

Serves 4

Soups and Garnishes

CROUTONS
(Kenyer Kockak)

3 tablespoons butter
3 slices white bread, toasted

Melt butter over low heat in a large, heavy skillet. Trim crust from toast and cut into 1/2-inch cubes. Put into skillet and stir until all sides are coated and golden in color. Remove from heat. Put in soup the last minutes before serving or serve on the side.

LIVER DUMPLINGS
(Maj Gomboc)

1/2 onion, finely chopped
2 tablespoons butter
3 to 4 chicken livers
1 teaspoon chopped parsley
1 teaspoon salt
1/2 teaspoon pepper
2 eggs
3 tablespoons bread crumbs
1 tablespoon all-purpose flour
1 slice white bread, moistened with milk
1 tablespoon butter

Brown onion in butter and set aside. Scrape livers with a knife to remove veins. Put in a bowl with all remaining ingredients. Let stand for 30 minutes.

Add dumplings to soup. (If mixture seems too soft, add more bread crumbs until balls hold their shape when dropped into boiling soup.) Let rise to the surface, cover, and simmer 5 minutes. Keep covered and hot until served.

These dumplings add flavor to any broth or ragout soup.

Serves 6

PINCHED NOODLES
(Csipetke)

3/4 cup all-purpose flour
1/2 teaspoon salt
1 tablespoon regular cream of wheat
1 egg

Combine flour, salt, and cream of wheat. Break egg into center of the flour mixture. Stir to make a stiff dough. Knead with your hands until smooth. Pinch off bits of the dough the size of hazelnuts and put them on a floured plate. When all the noodles are ready, drop into boiling soup. Cook about 10 minutes or until tender. Test for doneness by cutting a noodle open; if it is not floury inside, it is done.

My grandchildren have fun helping me make these noodles.

Serves 6

Soups and Garnishes

BUTTER DUMPLINGS
(Vajas Galuska)

3/4 cup all-purpose flour
1 egg
1 tablespoon butter, melted
1/4 cup milk
1 tablespoon finely chopped parsley
1 tablespoon regular cream of wheat

Combine all ingredients. Let stand 30 minutes. Dip spoon into boiling soup, then cut off small piece of the dough. Dip spoon into soup and dough will come off.

When all dumplings are in the pot, lower heat to simmering. Let dumplings rise to the surface, cover and simmer 2 to 3 minutes.

Serves 6

CREAM OF WHEAT DUMPLINGS
(Dara Galuska)

10 cups water with 1 teaspoon salt
1 large egg, separated
1-1/2 teaspoons salt
1/2 cup regular cream of wheat

Bring water and salt to a boil. Beat egg white until stiff; fold in egg yolk, salt, and cream of wheat. Form a dumpling with a teaspoon, and drop into simmering water. If the dumpling does not hold its shape, add 1 to 2 teaspoons cream of wheat to the batter.

When all dumplings are in the pot, cover and maintain a rolling boil. Cook dumplings 8 to 10 minutes. Carefully remove with slotted spoon and put into simmering soup broth. Simmer 10 more minutes. The dumplings are excellent in chicken or beef broth.

These dumplings are my grandchildren's favorites; I never seem to cook enough for them.

Serves 4 to 6

GOLDEN DROPS
(Csurgatott Teszta)

1 egg
1/2 cup milk
3/4 to 1 cup all-purpose flour,
    depending on size of egg
1 teaspoon salt
1 tablespoon butter, melted
1 tablespoon regular cream of wheat
vegetable oil for deep frying

Combine all ingredients except oil to make a very thick dough. Put dough through the "wrong" side of a round-holed grater into a pot of hot oil. The oil should be at least 3 inches deep. Stir dough with a soup spoon. When the dough becomes golden in color, take it out with a slotted spoon and put in a bowl lined with paper towel.

This is one of the best and most elegant garnishes for any clear or creamed soup.

Serves 6

Hors d'Oeuvre

Hungarians believe that love, music, and food are the three ingredients essential to happiness. Thus, great importance is placed on hospitality.

When entertaining, the first impression should create an atmosphere of warmth and cordiality. Thus the emphasis on the appetizer. Many of the appetizers I have included can be served as a complete meal; others are more appropriate as a first course to be served at the table or in the living room, as a finger food.

I want to express my hospitality by sharing some of my family recipes with you. You can be assured they are well tested, so be my guests! And I hope you will have a good time.

Hors d'Oeuvre

WARM CHEESE DIP
(Meleg Sajt Martogatos)

1 large onion, finely chopped
2 tablespoons butter, melted
1 garlic clove, finely chopped
1 16-ounce can stewed tomatoes
1 6-ounce can green chili peppers, diced
1-1/2 pounds sharp cheddar cheese, grated

Brown onion in butter until golden. Add garlic and gradually add the tomatoes and chili peppers. Add cheese and simmer for 10 minutes, stirring occasionally. If you would like a spicier dip, add green chili salsa (sauce) to taste.

When ready to use, heat in a double boiler and serve hot in a chafing dish.

If the entire dip is not used, a portion can be frozen for later use.

This recipe was given to be by my daughter, Panni. We constantly exchange our recipes with one another.

Makes 3 to 4 cups

HUNGARIAN CHEESE SPREAD
(Korozott)

1 8-ounce package cream cheese
1/4 pound butter
3 tablespoons sour cream
3 to 4 green onions, including stalk, chopped
1 tablespoon prepared mustard
2 teaspoons Hungarian paprika
1 to 1-1/2 teaspoons caraway seeds
1/2 teaspoon salt
1/4 pound feta cheese (optional)
2 anchovy filets and 1 teaspoon capers for garnish

Bring cream cheese and butter to room temperature. Put in a bowl along with the remaining ingredients; blend well. Transfer mixture to a serving plate and shape into a smooth mound. If desired, mold into the shape of an artichoke using a spoon dipped in hot water. Garnish with anchovies and capers.

In Hungary we always made this spread with sheep's cheese. Feta cheese can be added to the spread to get closer to the flavor of the traditional Hungarian recipe.

Variation: To use as a dip, add more sour cream and serve in a bowl. Save some of the green onion for garnish.

Radishes are very good with this spread, along with crackers and pumpernickel or rye bread.

Makes 1-1/2 to 2 cups

CHOPPED CHICKEN LIVER
(Csirke Maj Vagdalva)

1 small onion, finely chopped
4 tablespoons butter or bacon drippings
1 pound chicken livers
2 hard-boiled eggs, finely chopped
salt and white pepper to taste
prepared mustard to taste
white or rye toast

Brown onion in butter or bacon drippings until golden. Add chicken liver and sauté 5 minutes, stirring constantly. Remove onion and liver from heat. Chop liver and onion and combine with eggs and seasonings.

Trim crust from white or rye toast and cut in triangles. Lightly butter and serve warm with chicken liver.

Variation: The chicken liver can also be put in an an aspic garnished with olives, hard-boiled eggs, capers or pimientos.

Makes 1-1/2 to 2 cups

HERRING DIP
(Hering Martogato)

3 tablespoons ground, slivered almonds
1 teaspoon prepared mustard
1/2 teaspoon prepared horseradish
few drops lemon juice
few drops Worcestershire sauce
white pepper to taste
2 to 3 mild pickled herrings in wine sauce, minced
1/2 cup heavy cream, whipped

Combine almonds, mustard, horseradish, lemon juice, Worcestershire, and pepper. Blend well and add herring. Last fold in whipped cream.

Serve cold with buttered bread fingers or crackers.

Makes 1 to 1-1/2 cups

Hors d'Oeuvre

TASTY SPREAD FOR COCKTAILS OR TEA
(Keno Sajtos Keverek)

1/4 pound butter, room temperature
1/4 pound Swiss cheese, grated
1/4 pound ground salami
2 hard-boiled eggs, chopped
anchovy paste and prepared mustard to taste
anchovies and olives for garnish

Combine butter, cheese, salami, and eggs. Put through a sieve or purée in a blender. Add anchovy paste and mustard to taste.

Rinse a mold or bowl with cold water and put mixture into it, making sure to press against the sides to keep the shape of the mold. Refrigerate 2 to 3 hours.

When ready to serve, put under hot water for 1 to 2 minutes and turn out on a large platter. Garnish with anchovies and olives. Serve with crackers and deviled eggs.

Makes 1 to 1-1/2 cups

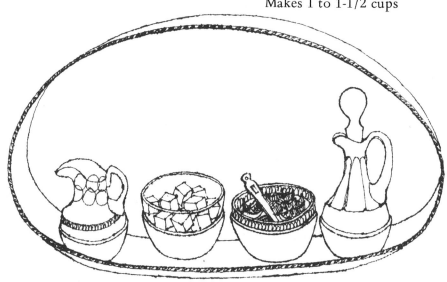

PÂTÉ
(Pastetom)

1 pound ground calf's liver
1/4 pound ground veal
1/2 pound ground pork
1 onion, finely chopped
2 tablespoons bacon drippings
6 to 8 anchovy filets
3 eggs
1-1/2 cups cream
salt and pepper to taste
3 to 4 slices fat pork or bacon

Put calf's liver, veal, and pork through a grinder or blender to grind fine. Sauté onion in bacon drippings and put through grinder or blender, along with the anchovies. Combine eggs with cream, salt, and pepper. Blend well and gradually add to the meat and onion mixture.

Line a mold with the fat pork or bacon slices and fill 3/4 full with the pâté mixture. Set in a shallow pan with 1 to 2 inches warm water. Bake at 350° for 2 to 2-1/2 hours.

Let cool and refrigerate overnight. Serve on a platter with lettuce and deviled eggs.

STEAMED LIVER PÂTÉ
(Gozolt Maj Pastetom)

1/4 pound butter
4 green onions, finely chopped
1/4 pound mushrooms, finely chopped
1 clove garlic, finely chopped
1/4 cup minced parsley
8 slices white bread, soaked in milk
1-1/2 pounds chicken livers
4 eggs, well beaten
salt and pepper to taste

Melt butter in a large frying pan. Add green onions and brown until golden. Add mushrooms, garlic, parsley, bread, and half of the chicken liver, mashed. Add eggs and stir constantly until set. Add second half of liver, sliced.

Put in a well-buttered meat-loaf dish. Set in a shallow pan with 1 to 2 inches hot water. Bake in a 350° oven for 1-1/2 to 2 hours.

Let cool and turn out on a platter. This is the best substitute for goose liver pâté.

Hors d'Oeuvre

HOT BEEF MARROW ON TOAST
(Csontvelo Piritoson)

I would like to mention another specialty of our meals which is served with soup. This is hot beef marrow from the bones used to make beef broth. Spread the marrow on hot toast and sprinkle with salt and paprika. You will find this is another delicacy of our menus.

HAM PÂTÉ
(Sonka Pastetom)

2 cups chicken broth
1 envelope gelatin
1 pound ground ham
1 egg
4 to 5 anchovy filets
1 tablespoon finely chopped capers
1-1/2 cups heavy cream
salt and pepper to taste
prepared mustard to taste
1/2 cup basic white sauce (see page 53)

Make an aspic by dissolving the gelatin in the chicken broth.

Combine all the remaining ingredients and mix well. Line the bottom of an oiled mold with aspic and refrigerate. When layer is set, put garnishes of your choice on it (hard-boiled egg slices, olives, pickle slices). Add more aspic and let set.

Spoon the ham mixture into the center of the mold, leaving space around the edge. Fill sides and top with aspic.

This pâté is tastier if refrigerated 1 day before serving.

PICKLED VEAL ROULADES
WITH GREEN SAUCE
(Pacolt Borju Tekeres Zold Martassal)

Veal Roulades
4 slices veal steak
salt to taste
1/2 pound mushrooms, finely chopped
1 green onion, finely chopped
parsley to taste
4 tablespoons butter
salt and pepper to taste
3 eggs, slightly beaten

Marinade
2 tablespoons white vinegar
salt to taste
1 peppercorn
1 bay leaf
1 carrot, chopped
1 stalk celery, chopped
water to cover

Sauce
1 cup mayonnaise
salt to taste
sugar to taste
prepared mustard to taste
lemon juice to taste
1 drop green food coloring

Pound veal slices until thin and sprinkle with salt. Sauté mushrooms, onion, and parsley in melted butter. Season with salt and pepper. Add eggs, stirring until set.

Cool mixture and spread over veal slices. Roll up and fasten with string. Combine ingredients for marinade in a large saucepan and bring to boil. Add veal roulades and simmer until meat is tender. Let cool in marinade overnight.

When ready to serve, slice and serve with green mayonnaise sauce.

Combine ingredients for sauce. Arrange veal roulades on a large platter with shredded lettuce and deviled eggs. Garnish meat with a few spoonfuls of the sauce; serve the remaining sauce in a gravy boat.

Serves 6 to 8

Hors d'Oeuvre

BAKED STUFFED MUSHROOMS
(Toltott Gomba Sulve)

12 large mushrooms
1 clove garlic, minced
4 tablespoons butter
3 tablespoons minced parsley
2 tablespoons minced walnuts
1/2 cup bread crumbs
2 eggs, slightly beaten
butter
pimiento strips for garnish

Carefully remove the stems from the mushroom caps; finely mince stems and sauté with the garlic in melted butter for 5 minutes. Mix in the parsley, nuts, bread crumbs, and eggs. Stuff the caps with mixture.

Place a dot of butter on each cap and bake in a greased dish at 350° for 15 minutes. Garnish each cap with a strip of pimiento. Keep warm in a chafing dish.

Serves 6

STUFFED MUSHROOMS WITH MEAT
(Hussal Toltott Gomba)

15 medium-sized mushrooms
1/2 pound ground beef
1/2 onion, finely chopped
1/4 green pepper, finely chopped
2 tablespoons chopped almonds
2 tablespoons bread crumbs
1 teaspoon Worcestershire sauce
1 tablespoon white vinegar
1 egg, slightly beaten
2 tablespoons butter

Remove stems from the mushrooms and finely chop stems. Combine the stems, ground beef, onion, green pepper, almonds, bread crumbs, Worcestershire, vinegar, and egg.

Sauté the mushroom caps lightly on both sides in butter. Place on a baking sheet or chafing dish. Mix the butter remaining in the skillet with the stuffing and fill the caps. If you use a baking sheet, put a dot of butter on each mushroom. Broil for 5 minutes, 3 inches below the flame, or cook and keep hot in a chafing dish.

Serves 6 to 12

Hors d'Oeuvre

MUSHROOM CASSEROLE
(Larakott Gomba)

13 large mushrooms
4 green onions, finely chopped
4 tablespoons butter
3 tablespoons all-purpose flour
heavy cream to thicken
salt and pepper to taste
butter
grated cheese, bread crumbs, and
   paprika for garnish

    Wash mushrooms quickly in salted water and wipe dry; clean and remove stems. Sauté onions in butter. Add stems and one mushroom, chopped and cook until brown. Sprinkle flour over pan and add enough cream to make a thick, creamy sauce. Add salt and pepper to taste.
    Place mushroom caps in baking dish and pour mixture over the top. Dot with butter and sprinkle generously with grated cheese and bread crumbs. Sprinkle lightly with paprika.
    Bake in a 350° oven for 20 minutes, then put under the broiler for 1 to 2 minutes.
    This is a very elegant side dish for any meat course, as well as an outstanding hors d'oeuvre.
    Serves 6 to 8

CHEESE-HAM CROQUETTES
(Sajtos Sonkas Krokett)

2 tablespoons butter
1 teaspoon chopped parsley
1/4 cup all-purpose flour
1 cup milk, warm
3 tablespoons chopped ham
1/2 cup grated Parmesan cheese
1 egg, well beaten
vegetable oil for deep frying

Coating
1/2 cup all-purpose flour
1 to 2 eggs
1/2 cup bread crumbs

    Melt butter in a saucepan; add parsley and stir 2 to 3 minutes; add flour and stir mixture until it bubbles. Slowly add milk, stirring constantly until smooth.
    Remove from heat and mix in ham, cheese, and beaten egg. Cool and shape into croquettes or balls. Roll in flour, dip in egg, and roll in bread crumbs.
    Deep fry in hot oil. This is an excellent side dish for any fish or meat course. If served by itself, cover with mushroom sauce (see page 54).

ZIPPY CHICKEN WITH DIP
(Csirke Szarny Martassal)

20 to 30 chicken wings

Marinade
soy sauce to taste
white wine to taste
salt and pepper to taste

Dip
1/2 cup mayonnaise
1/3 cup pickle relish
2 hard-boiled eggs, finely chopped
salt, pepper, and dill weed to taste

Use only meaty, upper part of chicken wing. Marinate wings in soy sauce, wine, salt, and pepper for 2 hours. Broil each side 5 to 10 minutes or until tender. Cool.

Combine all ingredients for dip. Put dip in a bowl surrounded by cold chicken wings.

This is a very appetizing finger food.

Count at least 3 wings per person

CHICKEN WINGS MADE À LA PANNI
(Csirke Szarny Panni Modra)

18 to 20 chicken wings
1 cup soy sauce
1/4 cup dry white wine
1 small piece ginger root, grated
1/2 teaspoon garlic powder
1 teaspoon sugar

Use only upper, meaty part of the wing (the lower section can be saved for soup).

Combine soy sauce, wine, ginger root, garlic powder, and sugar. Marinate chicken wings in mixture for 3 to 4 hours. Preheat oven to 450°. Drain wings well and put on greased baking dish. Bake for 10 minutes; turn and bake for 30 minutes, turning heat down to 350° and draining off liquid if required.

If added crispness is desired, put wings under broiler for several minutes before serving. Put foil or paper collar on each piece so that it is easy to pick up in your fingers. Serve hot.

This is also one of my daughter's tasty recipes.

Serves 6

Hors d'Oeuvre

HUNGARIAN MEATBALLS
(Magyaros Hus Gombocok)

1 pound ground round
1/2 onion, finely chopped
1/2 green pepper, finely chopped
4 tablespoons chopped almonds
2 tablespoons bread crumbs
1 egg
2 tablespoons butter
1 tablespoon white vinegar
1 teaspoon Worcestershire sauce
parsley and salt to taste

Combine all ingredients and shape into small balls the size of a walnut.

Gravy
4 tablespoons butter
1 onion, finely chopped
1 tablespoon Hungarian paprika
1/2 tomato, finely chopped
1/2 green pepper, chopped
salt to taste
1 cup water

Melt butter in a skillet; add onion and brown, stirring constantly. Add paprika, tomato, green pepper, and salt. Mix and add water. When gravy starts cooking, add the tiny meatballs and simmer covered for 30 minutes. If necessary, add more water. Put a toothpick in each meatball and serve in a chafing dish.

I assure you this is a most tasty hors d'oeuvre. One year my daughter had a New Year's Eve party with a great spread of fine foods. Of all the food, the meatballs were the most popular. My two grandsons were excellent helpers. I promised them 25 cents for every 100 meatballs they made. One said it was more fun than making mud balls.

Serves 6

EGGS WITH MUSHROOMS
(Gombas Tojas)

4 tablespoons butter
3 green onions, finely chopped
1/2 pound mushrooms, washed and sliced
1/4 cup minced parsley
salt and pepper to taste
6 eggs
parsley and paprika for garnish

Melt butter in a large frying pan. Add green onions and brown until golden. Add mushrooms and parsley and sauté covered for 3 to 4 minutes. Combine salt, pepper, and eggs and beat well; add to the pan and stir until desired consistency. Remove from heat and serve immediately. Garnish with parsley and paprika.

Variation: Mushroom Omelette If you would like an omelette, don't stir eggs while cooking. Occasionally loosen edges and bottom of pan with a spatula, allowing uncooked part of the egg to flow to the bottom. Cook until eggs are thick and creamy throughout, but still moist. Put sautéed mushrooms in the middle of the omelette. When cooked, fold half of the omelette over mushrooms. Garnish with paprika or grated cheese. Serve immediately on a hot platter.

Serves 4

HUNGARIAN EGG FRITTERS
(Kirantott Tojas)

6 hard-boiled eggs
1 to 2 raw eggs
salt and pepper to taste
1/2 cup bread crumbs
vegetable oil for deep frying
chopped chives or parsley for garnish
6 pieces toast

Cut the hard-boiled eggs in half lengthwise. Beat raw egg and mix with salt and pepper. Dip hard-boiled eggs in raw egg mixture and roll in bread crumbs.

Fry in hot oil until golden. (Oil must be at least 3 inches deep.) Garnish with chives or parsley. Serve on hot buttered toast.

Serves 6

Hors d'Oeuvre

EGGS WITH GREEN PEPPERS
(Zoldpaprikas Rantotta)

3 firm green peppers
4 tablespoons butter
6 eggs, well beaten
salt to taste
paprika and tomato slices for garnish

Wash and clean peppers, discarding seeds. Slice crosswise in 1-inch strips.

Melt butter in large frying pan. Add sliced peppers and sauté covered for 10 to 15 minutes or until tender.

Combine salt and eggs and add to the pan, stirring gently until eggs are set. Serve immediately. Garnish with tomato slices and paprika.

Variation: Sauté an onion in the melted butter before adding green pepper. Add sliced sausage to the pan before adding the eggs.

Serves 4

CHEESE SOUFFLÉ
(Sajt Felfujt)

8 ounces Velveeta cheese
1/2 cup half-and-half
6 eggs, separated
1 teaspoon salt
grated Parmesan cheese

Combine cheese and half-and-half. Put in a double boiler over low heat and stir until cheese is melted. Combine egg yolks and salt and beat well. Add to the cheese mixture. Carefully fold in well-beaten, stiff, egg whites.

Generously butter a baking dish or a soufflé dish and sprinkle insides well with grated cheese. Make a foil collar around the top of the dish and fasten with a pin. This gives the soufflé room to rise above the dish. Bake at 325° for 25 to 30 minutes. Since a soufflé must be served immediately, wait until all guests have arrived before putting it in the oven. The guests can wait, but the soufflé can't!

Variation: Soufflé au Jambon Add 1/2 cup finely diced, cooked ham in with the cheese and half-and-half mixture.

Variation: Soufflé aux Épinards Add 1/2 cup cooked, drained, finely chopped spinach into the cheese and half-and-half mixture.

Serves 6

BRAIN SOUFFLÉ
(Velos Pudding)

1 beef brain
1/2 onion, finely chopped
1/4 pound butter
5 eggs, separated
1 tablespoon minced parsley
salt and pepper to taste
3 tablespoons bread crumbs
grated Parmesan cheese or mushroom
    sauce (see page 54) for garnish

Put brain in boiling water 2 to 3 minutes; drain and remove membrane. Put through a sieve. Brown onion in 1/3 of the butter. Beat egg yolks and mix with remaining butter, brain, parsley, salt, pepper, and cooled browned onion. Add well-beaten, stiff egg whites alternately with bread crumbs.

Put in well-greased soufflé mold with a tight-fitting lid and place in boiling water. Cook 30 to 35 minutes. Serve immediately with grated Parmesan cheese or mushroom sauce.

I know Americans often find brains distasteful but if you are brave enough to try them, you will soon consider them one of the finest of gourmet dishes.

Serves 4 to 6

DEVILED EGGS
(Toltott Tojas)

In my recipes I often suggest using deviled eggs for decoration or as a side dish.

Put eggs in cold water, bring to boil and allow to boil 3 to 4 minutes. Cool 2 to 3 minutes in the cooking water and transfer to cold water and cool completely. Peel egg and cut crosswise (not lengthwise); remove yolk. Cut off the tip of the egg so it sits flat and mix with the yolk, mayonnaise, salt, and pepper. Anchovy paste, ground ham, or crumbled bacon can also be added. Stuff eggs.

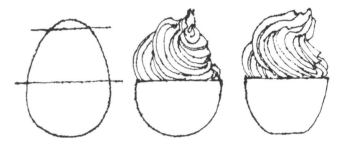

Salads

In Hungary salad is served with the main course as a side dish. When I go to an American restaurant, I try to save some of my salad to have with the main course. However, I seldom go to a restaurant anymore, as my family and my friends discovered long ago that the best food and nicest meals are prepared at home.

Lettuce season is from early spring until late fall. Therefore Hungarian pantries are filled with a variety of preserves to replace the salads for winter: homemade pickles, peppers, spiced prunes, sour cherries, and peaches line the shelves in huge jars. In my pantry each had a paper cup on the top labeled with the date of canning. It was very picturesque and appetizing to see the different colors and shapes on the well-stocked shelves.

Salads

CUCUMBER SALAD
(Uborka Salata)

3 cucumbers, pared and thinly sliced
2 teaspoons salt
3 tablespoons white vinegar
3 tablespoons water
1 tablespoon sugar
1/2 teaspoon Hungarian paprika
1/4 teaspoon pepper
green pepper rings and tomato slices for garnish

Place cucumbers in a bowl and sprinkle with salt. Set aside for 1 to 1-1/2 hours. Meanwhile, combine vinegar, water, and sugar and set aside.

When cucumbers have set, squeeze with your hand to remove liquid. Put squeezed cucumbers in a salad bowl and pour the vinegar mixture over; toss lightly. Sprinkle with paprika and pepper. Garnish with green pepper rings and tomato slices.

Variation: Creamed Cucumber Salad Add 1/2 cup sour cream to vinegar dressing.
Serves 4 to 6

CABBAGE SALAD
(Kaposzta Salata)

1 large head cabbage, thinly sliced
1 onion, sliced
2 tablespoons salt
1-1/2 tablespoons sugar
1/2 cup water
1/2 cup white vinegar
1 teaspoon freshly ground black pepper
green pepper rings and tomato slices for garnish

Put cabbage and onion in a bowl and sprinkle with salt. Combine sugar, water, and vinegar in a bowl. When cabbage is limp, squeeze with your hand to remove juice and drain. Put cabbage in vinegar mixture and turn until well coated with dressing. Sprinkle with pepper and garnish with tomato slices and green pepper rings. Serve well chilled.

This salad is tastier if prepared a day ahead and chilled overnight.
Serves 6

TOMATO SALAD
(Paradicsom Salata)

1 pound tomatoes
2 tablespoons white vinegar
1 tablespoon water
1/2 teaspoon salt
1 teaspoon sugar
1 teaspoon salad oil
1/2 teaspoon ground black pepper
1 tablespoon finely chopped chives
1/2 tablespoon minced parsley

Dip tomatoes in hot water, peel, and slice. Make dressing by combining vinegar, water, salt, sugar, and oil. Pour over nicely arranged tomato slices. Sprinkle with ground pepper and garnish with chives and parsley. Chill before serving.

Almost any vegetable—green beans, kidney beans, asparagus, cauliflower—which is already cooked can be made into a fine salad using the same dressing as above. Leftover meat and fish can also be used. Cut in strips and toss in dressing. Garnish with onion rings. If desired, add 1 to 2 tablespoons of mayonnaise to the dressing.

Serves 6

CELERY ROOT SALAD
(Zeller Salata)

1 large celery root
1/2 cup white vinegar
1/2 cup water
1 to 2 bay leaves
6 to 8 peppercorns
4 to 6 coriander seeds
salt and sugar to taste

Wash celery root well. Peel and wash again. Put in salted, boiling water to cover. Cook until tender. Save the cooking water and use as a stock for potato soup (see page 19).

Prepare marinade by combining vinegar, water, bay leaves, peppercorns, coriander seeds, salt, and sugar. Slice cooked celery root and put in marinade.

This salad can be put in a large jar and refrigerated until ready to serve.

Serves 6

Salads

POTATO SALAD WITH CELERY ROOT
(Krumpli Salata)

4 medium-sized potatoes
1 medium-sized celery root
1 onion, thinly sliced
4 tablespoons white vinegar
4 tablespoons water
1 teaspoon salt
sugar to taste
2 hard-boiled eggs for garnish

Cook washed potatoes and celery root in salted, boiling water until tender. Peel and slice thin. Combine onion slices with potatoes and celery root. Make dressing by mixing vinegar, water, salt, and sugar; pour over salad. Toss gently and garnish with sliced, hard-boiled eggs.

Serves 6

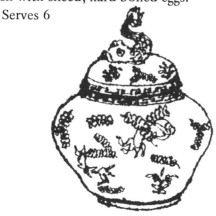

CREAMED POTATO SALAD
(Tejfolos Krumpli Salata)

4 medium-sized potatoes
1 teaspoon salt
2 tablespoons white vinegar
2 tablespoons water
3 tablespoons mayonnaise
3 tablespoons sour cream
1/2 teaspoon white pepper
2 tablespoons sweet relish
1 tablespoon sugar
1 teaspoon prepared mustard
2 to 3 green onions, finely chopped
2 hard-boiled eggs
green pepper slices and green olives

Cook potatoes in salted, boiling water until tender; cool, peel, and dice. Sprinkle with salt and a mixture of the vinegar and water.

In another bowl combine mayonnaise, sour cream, pepper, relish, sugar, mustard, and green onions. Taste and correct seasoning. Add potatoes to the dressing and mix. Let stand for 2 to 3 hours and taste. If necessary, correct seasoning again. Toss gently and garnish with grated hard-boiled eggs, green pepper rings, and several green olives.

Serves 6

GREEN OR RED BELL PEPPER SALAD
(Paprika Salata)

1 to 1-1/2 pounds green or red bell peppers
3 tablespoons water
2 teaspoons sugar
1 teaspoon salt
3 tablespoons white vinegar

Wash and core bell peppers. Scald and slice into rings. Combine water, sugar, salt, and vinegar; pour over bell pepper rings. Let stand a few hours before serving.

The use of bell peppers became more important when their vitamin C content was discovered by Dr. Szentgyorgyi, Hungary's Nobel Prize winner.

Serves 6

PICKLED BEET SALAD
(Cekla Salata)

2 pounds beets, washed (pick out beets that
   are the same size)
2 tablespoons white vinegar
2 tablespoons water
1 teaspoon salt
1 tablespoon sugar
1/2 teaspoon caraway seeds
1 teaspoon prepared horseradish

Cook beets in skins until tender. Peel and cut in thin slices. Mix remaining ingredients and pour over sliced beets. Let stand several hours. Keep in a jar in the refrigerator until ready to serve.

If you would like beets to be an interesting pink color, add 1 tablespoon mayonnaise to the dressing before serving.

Serves 8

Salads

RAW VEGETARIAN SALAD
(Vegetarianus Salata)

1/2 pound red cabbage, washed and shredded
1/2 pound celery root, washed, peeled, and
   finely shredded
1/2 pound carrots, washed, peeled, and
   finely shredded
1/2 beet, washed and finely shredded
1/2 pound cauliflower, washed and finely chopped
1/2 pound spinach, washed and finely chopped
1/2 pound radishes, washed and finely chopped
radishes and parsley for garnish

Dressing
1 pint sour cream
1/2 cup half-and-half
1 teaspoon dill weed
1 teaspoon finely chopped parsley
2 teaspoons finely chopped chives
salt and sugar to taste
lemon juice and several drops of
   vegetable oil to taste

Put vegetables through a grater, keeping each
vegetable separate; sprinkle lightly with salt. Let
stand for 1 hour then squeeze out excess liquid.
Combine dressing ingredients and add desired
amount to each vegetable. Still keeping vegetables
separate, place on a large platter, alternating colors.
Garnish with radishes and parsley.

   Serves 8

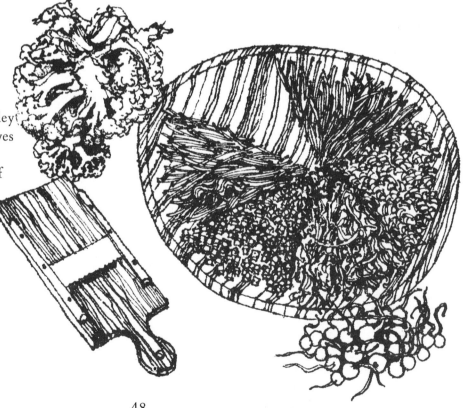

MIXED VEGETABLE SALAD
PARISIAN STYLE
(Francia Salata)

3 to 4 carrots, peeled and washed
1 potato, unpeeled and washed
1 celery root, peeled and washed, or
   2 stalks celery
1/2 cup peas
1 apple, peeled and diced
1 pickle, diced
2 hard-boiled eggs, diced
1/2 cup mayonnaise
1/2 cup sour cream
1 teaspoon prepared mustard
1 teaspoon sugar
1 teaspoon salt
1 teaspoon capers
1 hard-boiled egg, sliced, for garnish

Boil separately in water carrots, potatoes, celery root, and peas; do not overcook. Dice carrots and celery root, and peel and dice potato. Combine with peas, apple, pickle, and hard-boiled eggs. Combine mayonnaise, sour cream, mustard, sugar, salt, and capers and pour over vegetables. Toss gently and garnish with hard-boiled egg.

Vegetables used in making broth can also be used to make this salad. It is a tasty salad to serve with cold cuts.

Serves 6

FRUIT SALAD
(Gyumolcs Salata)

4 cups combined fresh fruits of your choice
   (If bananas, peaches, or pears are used, dip
   pieces into lemon juice to prevent darkening.)
1/2 cup confectioner's sugar
4 tablespoons rum, cognac, or cointreau

Wash, peel and cut up fruit; place in a large salad bowl. Add sugar and toss gently. Chill in refrigerator for 1 hour. Pour liquor over just before serving. Serve in individual cocktail glasses or in a large bowl.

Serves 6

LETTUCE WITH LEMON DRESSING
(Citromos Salata)

juice of 1 lemon
2 tablespoons water
1 tablespoon sugar
1 teaspoon salt
1 head butter lettuce
2 ounces feta cheese
2 hard-boiled eggs, quartered

Combine the lemon juice, water, sugar, and salt to make dressing. Wash, drain, and trim lettuce. Put in a bowl and add dressing. Toss and add more seasoning to taste. Crumble feta cheese and put over the top. Garnish with egg quarters.

Serves 4

Salads

BASIC SALAD DRESSING
(Salatakhoz Alap Ontet)

3 tablespoons lemon juice
1/2 teaspoon dry mustard
1/2 teaspoon salt
sugar and pepper to taste
1/4 cup olive oil

Combine lemon juice, mustard, sugar, and pepper and mix well. Gradually add oil; beat well.

Variation: Add 1/2 tablespoon finely chopped capers, 1/2 tablespoon finely chopped chives, 1/2 tablespoon minced parsley, and 1 grated, hard-boiled egg. Serve with cold cuts.
Makes 3/4 to 1 cup

LETTUCE WITH MY FAVORITE DRESSING
(Salata Kedvene Modra)

1 head butter lettuce
2 hard-boiled eggs
1 tablespoon mayonnaise
2 tablespoons sour cream
1 teaspoon dry mustard
1 tablespoon white vinegar
1 teaspoon sugar
1/2 teaspoon salt
1/2 teaspoon seasoned salt (Lawry's)
1 green onion, finely chopped

Wash, drain, and trim lettuce; place in a large salad bowl. Grate egg whites and reserve for garnish. Mash egg yolks, combine with all other ingredients, and pour over lettuce. Toss. Garnish with grated egg whites.
Serves 4 to 6

HERRING SALAD
(Hering Salata)

3 herrings pickled in wine, sliced
3 hard-boiled eggs, sliced
2 apples, peeled and cubed
2 small potatoes, cooked in skin, peeled, and
    cubed
1 to 2 sweet pickles, finely chopped
juice of 1 lemon
1/4 cup salad oil
1/2 teaspoon white pepper
salt to taste
prepared mustard to taste
1/2 pint cream, whipped
lemon and orange wedges

Put herrings, eggs, apples, potatoes, and sweet pickles in a bowl. Add lemon juice, oil, pepper and, if desired, salt and a little mustard. Mix well. Let stand for 30 minutes and then add whipped cream before serving. Garnish with lemon and orange wedges. This can be served as a salad or an hors d'oeuvre.

Serves 6

DILL CUCUMBER
Pickled for Quick Use
(Kapros Uborka)

3 to 4 pounds medium-sized cucumbers
1/2 bunch fresh dill
1 to 2 cloves garlic, sliced
2 tablespoons salt
2 slices toast

Wash and score cucumbers; cut off ends. Put the fresh dill into a large, wide-necked preserving jar; then stand cucumbers up in the jar and sprinkle garlic in between; put toast over the top, add salt; finally add boiling water to cover.

Cover jar with paper with holes punched in the top; fasten with a rubber band. Let stand in a warm place for a week. Then remove bread from the jar and chill cucumbers. Even the strained juice from these cucumbers is refreshing and tasty to drink. Use in good health.

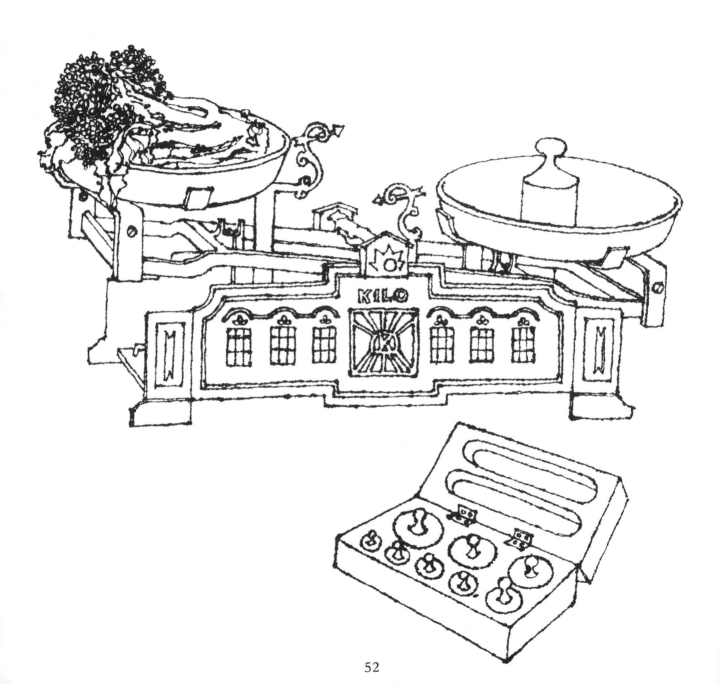

Sauces

Sauces are used much more frequently in continental cooking than in America. A well-chosen sauce turns the most simple dish into a gourmet meal. I am including some of my favorite sauces in this chapter. My son-in-law says that my seasoning is the best, but please correct and adjust the seasonings to your individual taste.

BASIC WHITE SAUCE
(Feher Martas Alap)

2 tablespoons butter
2 tablespoons all-purpose flour
1 cup cream or milk
salt and pepper to taste

Melt butter in saucepan over low heat. Stir in flour with a wooden spoon until mixture bubbles. Add liquid and stir until thick and smooth.

Variations: Add 1/2 cup grated, sharp cheddar cheese for cheese sauce. Chopped, cooked ham may also be added. These are good crêpe fillings.
Makes 1 cup

BÉCHAMEL SAUCE
(Krem Martas Alap)

3 tablespoons butter
1/4 teaspoon salt
1/4 teaspoon white pepper
3 tablespoons all-purpose flour
1 cup milk or cream
2 egg yolks

Melt butter in a double boiler. Mix together salt, pepper, and flour and add to melted butter. Gradually add milk, stirring constantly until thick. Add 4 tablespoons of the sauce to the egg yolks, stirring constantly until smooth. Return to double boiler and mix.

Variation: Add 1 teaspoon prepared mustard and a few drops of lemon juice to the sauce. This makes an excellent sauce for hot or cold vegetables.

Variation: Cold Pickle Sauce Add 1 teaspoon sugar and 1 finely chopped pickled cucumber to the Béchamel sauce and serve with cold or hot fish.
Makes about 1-1/2 cups

Sauces

TOMATO SAUCE
(Paradicsom Martas)

1 tablespoon butter
1 tablespoon all-purpose flour
1 8-ounce can tomato sauce
1 green onion
1 slice green pepper
1 stick cinnamon
1 to 2 cloves garlic
rind of 1/4 lemon
sugar and salt to taste

Melt butter in a saucepan. Stir in flour and simmer until mixture bubbles and is lightly browned. Add remaining ingredients and bring to a boil. Let simmer 10 to 15 minutes, stirring occasionally. Strain and serve hot with boiled meats or over rice. If too thick add some broth or half-and-half.
Makes about 1-1/2 cups

DELICIOUS MUSHROOM SAUCE
(Csoda Gomba Martas)

1 pound white mushrooms
3 tablespoons butter
3 green onions, chopped
1/4 cup minced parsley
1 to 2 bouillon cubes
1/2 pint sour cream
3 tablespoons all-purpose flour
1/2 cup water
1/2 teaspoon salt
1/2 teaspoon pepper

Soak mushrooms in cold, salted water 3 to 4 minutes, changing water several times and rubbing mushrooms with your hands. Remove from water and drain well.

Cut away the end of the mushroom stems and slice mushrooms. Melt butter in a large saucepan. Add green onions and sauté until golden. Add sliced mushrooms, parsley, and bouillon cube. Simmer 2 to 3 minutes, covered.

Combine sour cream and flour; stir with a whisk until smooth. Gradually add water, salt, and pepper. Stir into saucepan with mushrooms. Simmer several minutes. Do not cook too long or the delicate flavor of the mushrooms will be lost.

If the sauce is too thick, add a little white wine. Mushroom sauce may be served with boiled meats, hot entrées, or with braised chops.
Serves 6 to 8

DILL SAUCE
(Kapor Martas)

2 tablespoons butter
2 tablespoons all-purpose flour
1/2 cup beef broth
1 tablespoon white vinegar
1 teaspoon sugar
1/2 teaspoon salt
1 tablespoon chopped, fresh dill
1/2 cup sour cream

Melt butter in a saucepan. Stir in flour and simmer until mixture bubbles and is lightly browned. Gradually add beef broth, vinegar, sugar, salt, and dill. Simmer 2 to 3 minutes. Add sour cream and serve with boiled meat.

Makes about 1-1/2 cups

GOOSEBERRY SAUCE
(Egres Martas)

1 16-ounce can gooseberries
2 eggs, well beaten
1/2 cup sugar
lemon juice (optional)

Put gooseberries in a saucepan and bring to a boil. Meanwhile, combine eggs and sugar; then gradually add gooseberries, stirring constantly. Chill and serve with hot or cold meat or fish.

Makes about 2 cups

HOT PICKLE SAUCE
(Uborka Martas)

1-1/2 tablespoons butter
1-1/2 tablespoons all-purpose flour
1 teaspoon sugar
1 cup beef broth, or 1 cup water and
   1 bouillon cube
3 medium-sized, pickled cucumbers,
   peeled and cubed
salt and sugar to taste
2 tablespoons sour cream
white vinegar to taste (optional)

Melt butter in saucepan. Stir in flour and sugar and simmer until mixture bubbles. Add beef broth, cucumber, salt, sugar, and sour cream. If desired, add a little vinegar. Boil for 2 to 3 minutes and serve hot with boiled beef.

Makes about 1-1/2 cups

Sauces

MAYONNAISE WITHOUT OIL
(Olaj Nelkuli Mayonnaise)

2 eggs
1-1/2 cups sour cream
1 tablespoon butter
salt and sugar to taste
lemon juice to taste
prepared mustard to taste
1/2 cup cream

Put eggs and sour cream in a double boiler over low heat and beat constantly until thick. Remove from heat and add butter. Cool and add seasonings to taste. Add cream and serve. If a green sauce is desired, add a drop of green food coloring or a tablespoon of spinach juice.

This is an excellent basic sauce for all kinds of cold meats, salads, and hard-boiled eggs.

Makes about 2 cups

CHESTNUT SAUCE
(Gesztenye Martas)

1/2 pound chestnuts
2 tablespoons butter
2 tablespoons all-purpose flour
1 cup beef broth, or 1 cup water and
　　1 bouillon cube
1/2 teaspoon sugar
1/2 teaspoon salt

Cook chestnuts for 5 minutes in boiling water. Peel away outside and inside skin and cut into small cubes.

Melt butter in a saucepan. Stir in flour and simmer until mixture bubbles and is lightly browned. Add broth, chestnuts, sugar, and salt. Simmer 15 to 25 minutes.

This sauce is excellent with poultry or any kind of cooked meat.

Makes 1-1/2 to 2 cups

CELERY ROOT SAUCE
(Zeller Martas)

1 medium-sized celery root, washed and peeled
2 tablespoons butter
1 teaspoon sugar
2 tablespoons all-purpose flour
1 cup beef broth, or 1 cup water
   and 1 bouillon cube
1 tablespoon finely chopped parsley
salt

Peel celery fairly thick so all sandy part is removed. Wash well and cut into even, small cubes. Brown over low heat in melted butter until tender. Sprinkle sugar over celery root and stir. Sprinkle flour over and brown, stirring constantly. When lightly browned, add broth and parsley and let simmer 10 minutes. Add salt to taste. If the sauce is too thick, add more broth. This sauce is especially good with boiled turkey wings and with boiled chicken.

Makes 1-1/2 to 2 cups

HORSERADISH SAUCE
(Torma Martas)

1-1/2 tablespoons butter
2 tablespoons all-purpose flour
2 tablespoons grated horseradish, or
   1 tablespoon prepared horseradish
1/2 cup beef broth or 1 cup water
   with bouillon cube
2 tablespoons grated almonds
1/2 cup milk
1/2 teaspoon salt
1/2 teaspoon sugar

Melt butter in a saucepan. Stir in flour and simmer until mixture bubbles. Add horseradish, broth, almonds, and milk. Flavor to taste with salt and sugar. Generally served with cold meats or boiled beef.

Makes about 1-1/2 cups

Vegetables

In Hungary and most parts of Europe, the vegetables available vary with the seasons. Since we do not have fresh produce all year around, spring is very special with its fine, green vegetables. New potatoes and butter lettuce are quite a treat with young fried chicken; and fresh green peas and parsley in soup mean that spring has come.

We appreciate all the "primeurs"—the first vegetables of spring. We can as many of them as possible for winter use. In my pantry in Hungary, we had green beans, zucchini, peas, green pepper in tomato sauce for stuffed peppers, and cut-up tomatoes and green peppers called *lecso*. All the goulash dishes are seasoned with green pepper and tomato. If not in season, home-canned vegetables are used. We even dried parsley, since it is often used for flavoring vegetables. We never used ready-made canned vegetables.

As you will see, we often cream and spice our vegetables, making a simple dish more exciting.

Vegetables

CREAMED ZUCCHINI WITH DILL
(Tejfeles Tok Fozelek)

2 pounds zucchini
2 tablespoons white vinegar
1/2 cup water
1 teaspoon salt
2 tablespoons sugar
1-1/2 tablespoons butter
1-1/2 teaspoons dill weed
2 tablespoons all-purpose flour
4 tablespoons sour cream

Wash and slice zucchini into long julienne-like strips (if it is old or not tender, peel it as well). Put zucchini in a 3-quart pan. Add vinegar, water, salt, sugar, butter and half of the dill. Bring to a boil and simmer 8 to 10 minutes. Mix flour and sour cream and add to the zucchini, stirring constantly until the sauce thickens. When ready to serve, sprinkle the remaining dill over the vegetable.

I have a zucchini cutter which cuts the zucchini into long, julienne-like strips. You can find this special utensil in any fine cookware store.

Serves 6

STUFFED ZUCCHINI
(Toltott Tok)

4 medium-sized zucchini
3 slices white bread, cubed
2 green onions, chopped
1/4 cup chopped parsley
2 to 3 teaspoons grated cheddar cheese
salt and white pepper to taste
4 tablespoons butter
4 slices cheese for garnish

Cook unpeeled zucchini in boiling, salted water for several minutes, or until it begins to soften; don't overcook! Drain and let stand until cool enough to handle. Cut away ends and halve zucchini lengthwise. Scoop out centers with a spoon, chop pulp and mix with all remaining ingredients except butter.

Stuff zucchini halves with filling. Put a pat of butter on each zucchini half and place in a buttered baking dish. Bake at 375° for 30 minutes. Lay cheese strips on top. Bake 5 more minutes or until cheese is melted.

Serves 6

SPINACH SOUFFLÉ
(Spenot Pudding)

4 slices bacon
2 hard-boiled eggs, sliced
2 pounds fresh spinach, or
   2 10-ounce packages frozen spinach
4 eggs, separated
1 teaspoon salt
1/2 teaspoon pepper
3 tablespoons bread crumbs
1/2 cup grated cheddar cheese

Generously grease a 3-quart, round baking dish with butter. Crisscross bacon on the bottom of the dish, putting hard-boiled egg slices in between. Pour over this the following mixture.

Cook spinach, drain well, and chop. Beat the egg yolks and add to the spinach, along with salt, pepper, bread crumbs, and grated cheese. Beat egg whites until stiff and fold in.

Bake in a preheated oven at 400° about 35 minutes. Turn out on a flat, round platter and serve immediately.

This is a very tasty and decorative soufflé.

Serves 6

CREAMED SPINACH
(Spenot Pure)

2 pounds fresh spinach, or
   2 10-ounce packages frozen leaf spinach
1 clove garlic, cut in half
3 tablespoons butter
1 tablespoon all-purpose flour
1/2 pint heavy cream
1 bouillon cube
salt and pepper to taste
2 hard-boiled eggs, sliced

Cook frozen spinach as directed on package, adding garlic to the water. If the spinach is fresh, wash well and cook in unsalted water with garlic in an uncovered pot until tender. Drain well. Purée in a blender.

Melt butter in a saucepan and add flour, stirring until the mixture bubbles and is lightly browned. Add spinach, cream, bouillon cube, and salt and pepper to taste. Simmer for several minutes stirring constantly until well blended and thick. Garnish with hard-boiled eggs.

Serves 6 to 8

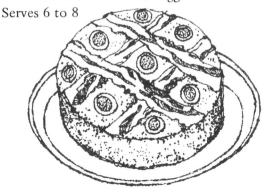

Vegetables

SPINACH ROULADE
(Spenot Tekercs)

2 pounds fresh spinach, well cleaned, or
   2 10-ounce packages frozen spinach
4 eggs, separated
1/2 pint sour cream
1-1/2 cups ground ham
4 tablespoons butter
salt and pepper to taste
grated Parmesan cheese

Cook the spinach in unsalted water over a high flame. Don't use lid. Drain, cool, and purée in a blender. Mix egg yolks and half of the sour cream and add to the spinach. Beat egg whites until stiff and fold in, along with 1/2 cup ham. Salt and pepper to taste.

Put foil on a baking sheet, grease well, and pour mixture over. Bake in 325° oven 40 to 45 minutes. Meanwhile, combine remaining ham and sour cream for filling.

When spinach is baked, remove from oven and lay out on a kitchen towel. Roll up in towel. After a few minutes, unroll and spread ham mixture over with a large knife. Reroll without the towel and sprinkle generously with grated cheese. Keep in a warm oven until ready to serve. This is a good main dish for lunch.

Variation: You can also vary the filling by using scrambled eggs and pouring mushroom sauce (see page 54) over the top.

Serves 6

CAULIFLOWER AU GRATIN
(Csoben Sult Karfiol)

1 medium-sized cauliflower
3 tablespoons butter
4 eggs, separated
salt to taste
1/2 pint sour cream
2 to 3 tablespoons bread crumbs
1/2 cup grated Parmesan cheese
1/2 teaspoon Hungarian paprika

Remove leaves and base from cauliflower. Stand in cold, salted water about 30 minutes; rinse. Cook in salted, boiling water 20 to 30 minutes or until tender but still firm.

Mix together butter, egg yolks, and salt. Blend in sour cream and bread crumbs and fold in well-beaten, stiff, egg whites.

Drain cauliflower, cool, and break into flowerettes. Pour smaller half of the egg mixture into a buttered casserole. Arrange cauliflower over the mixture; sprinkle with half of the Parmesan cheese and salt. Add the other half of the egg mixture; sprinkle with remaining Parmesan and paprika. Bake at 350° 30 minutes or until top is lightly browned.

This egg mixture is very practical for any vegetables. It also makes a successful new dish from leftover vegetables or meats.

Serves 4 to 6

CREAMED STRING BEANS
(Zoldbab Fozelek)

1 pound string beans
2/3 cup hot water
1 green onion, finely chopped
2 tablespoons butter
2 tablespoons all-purpose flour
4 tablespoons sour cream
salt, sugar, white vinegar, and parsley to taste

Wash beans, break off ends, and cut lengthwise several times. Simmer in water with the green onion and butter 15 to 20 minutes or until beans are tender. Mix flour and sour cream and add to the tender beans. Add salt, sugar, vinegar, and parsley to taste. Stir constantly for several minutes until well blended and thick.

Serves 4 to 6

EGGPLANT FRITTERS
(Kirantott Padlizsan)

1 large eggplant, unpeeled
2 eggs
2 cups all-purpose flour
1 cup milk
1 teaspoon salt
vegetable oil for deep frying
grated cheddar or Parmesan cheese

Slice eggplant in thin rounds, sprinkle with salt, and let stand 15 to 20 minutes. Mix egg, flour, milk, and salt. Wipe eggplant slices dry and dip into mixture. Deep fry in hot oil until golden. There should be at least 3 inches of oil in the pan.

Remove from pan and drain on absorbent paper. Sprinkle with grated cheese and serve immediately.

If you have leftover batter, it can be used to make golden drops (see page 25) for soups.

Serves 4 to 6

BAKED EGGPLANT
(Sult Padlizsan)

1 large eggplant, unpeeled
salt to taste
1/2 cup mayonnaise
1/2 cup grated cheddar or Parmesan cheese
1/2 cup bread crumbs
1 teaspoon salt
1 teaspoon Hungarian paprika

Slice eggplant in thin rounds, sprinkle with salt, and let stand for 15 to 20 minutes. Wipe dry and brush both sides with mayonnaise. Combine cheese, bread crumbs, and salt, and dip eggplant slices in mixture.

Put on a baking sheet and sprinkle with paprika. Bake in a 375° oven 8 to 10 minutes or until golden.

This is a very pleasant side dish for any roast.

Serves 4 to 6

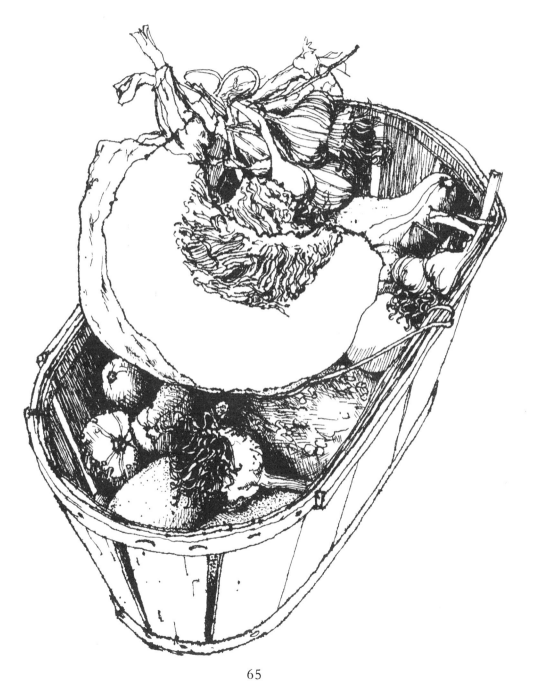

Vegetables

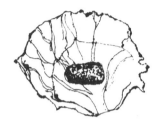

STUFFED CABBAGE
(Toltott Kaposzta)

3 tablespoons rice
1-1/2 pounds cabbage
4 slices bacon
1 large onion, chopped
1-1/2 pounds ground beef
1 egg
salt and pepper to taste
1 pound smoked short ribs
2 teaspoons Hungarian paprika
1 tomato, sliced
1 green pepper, sliced
2 pounds sauerkraut, washed and drained
1 potato, peeled and grated
1 apple, unpeeled and grated
1 teaspoon chopped lemon rind
2 bay leaves

Simmer rice in 5 tablespoons water for 10 minutes. Pour boiling water over cabbage, cover, and let stand 5 to 10 minutes; drain. Cool and carefully remove leaves one by one, trimming off the thick, heavy core.

Brown bacon in a heavy, 3-quart Dutch oven with a tight-fitting lid; remove and drain. Brown onion in the bacon drippings until transparent; remove part of the onion and combine with ground beef, egg, rice, salt, and pepper. Place a large tablespoon of this mixture on each cabbage leaf. Fold one end of the leaf over the meat, and roll up; tuck in well.

Put ribs in Dutch oven with bacon and remaining onion. Cover with water and simmer covered for 30 minutes. Add paprika, tomato, green pepper, sauerkraut, potato, apple, lemon rind, and bay leaves.

When sauerkraut begins to simmer, add the cabbage rolls to the pan, bring to a boil, reduce heat, and simmer covered for 1 to 1-1/2 hours.

When ready to serve, put sauerkraut on a large platter. Place ribs, cabbage rolls, and bacon on top.

In our vineyard in Hungary, the cabbage was prepared in barrels and pickled. This is a most popular Hungarian dish which tastes better each time it is reheated. It is often said that the seventh time is the best!

SAVOY CABBAGE ROLL WITH PÂTÉ
(Kelpastetom Tekercs)

1 pound veal shoulder, cut up
1/3 cup bacon drippings
5 eggs, separated
3/4 cup sour cream
3 tablespoons bread crumbs
salt, pepper, and seasoned salt to taste
1 2-pound head savoy cabbage
grated Parmesan cheese

Sauté veal in a covered pan on low heat in bacon drippings until tender. Cool and put through a grinder or purée in a blender. Mix egg yolks, sour cream, crumbs, and seasoning. Beat egg whites until stiff and fold in.

Pour boiling water over cabbage and let stand in hot water until leaves turn limp. Carefully peel off leaves and put on a kitchen towel in the shape of a rectangle. Mold meat mixture into a large, sausage shape, and put in the center of the leaves. Roll the leaves around the meat filling. Roll up in a kitchen towel and tie the ends of the towel with string. Put in a kettle of boiling water and cook 30 minutes. Roll out of towel onto a serving platter. Serve hot, generously sprinkled with grated Parmesan cheese.

Serves 6

Vegetables

SZEKELY LAYER CABBAGE
(Szekely Rakott Kaposzta)

2 pounds sauerkraut
1 pound ground pork
1 small onion, finely chopped
1 clove garlic, finely chopped
1 green pepper, chopped
salt and pepper to taste
4 slices bacon
1 cup cooked rice
4 smoked link sausages, sliced
6 smoked or fresh pork chops, sautéed in butter
1 pint sour cream
2 tablespoons half-and-half
1 tablespoon Hungarian paprika

Rinse and drain sauerkraut. Mix ground meat, onion, garlic, green pepper, and salt and pepper.

In a large oven casserole arrange layers as follows: bacon, sauerkraut, ground meat mixture, sauerkraut, rice and sausage, sauerkraut. Put pork chops and drippings on the top. Mix sour cream with half-and-half and pour over the top. Sprinkle with paprika and cover tightly. Bake at 350° 1-1/2 to 2 hours. Serve in the baking dish.

Serves 6 to 8

SZEKELY GOULASH
(Szekely Gulyas)

1 pound pork shoulder
1 pound pork ribs
2 tablespoons bacon drippings
1 large onion, chopped
1 tablespoon Hungarian paprika
1 tomato, chopped
1 green pepper, chopped
2 cloves garlic, finely chopped
1 teaspoon caraway seeds
2 pounds sauerkraut
1 pint sour cream
2 tablespoons all-purpose flour

Cut the pork into bite-sized cubes; slice the ribs. In a 3-quart Dutch oven or pot, sauté onion in bacon drippings until transparent. Add paprika, tomato, green pepper, garlic, caraway seeds, a little salt, and meat. Pour 1/2 cup water over and cover with a lid. Simmer about 1 hour, adding water as needed, until meat is tender.

Drain and rinse sauerkraut, saving the juice. Add sauerkraut to meat mixture and simmer 20 to 25 minutes. Mix sour cream and flour and add. Mix in some of the sauerkraut juice, if a tart flavor is desired. Transfer to a baking dish and bake in the oven at 300° 30 to 40 minutes.

This is a specialty of the southern part of Hungary, called Szekely.

Serves 6 to 8

BROCCOLI SOUFFLÉ RING
(Broccoly Soufflé)

1 bunch fresh broccoli
3/4 cup butter
5 tablespoons all-purpose flour
1 cup milk
6 eggs, separated
salt and pepper to taste
grated Parmesan cheese

Trim broccoli and steam until tender. Cut up into bite-sized pieces.

Melt butter in a large saucepan and stir in flour. When mixture bubbles, add milk and stir constantly until thick. Remove from flame and cool. Add egg yolks, one by one, stirring well. Add steamed broccoli, salt, and pepper. Beat egg whites until stiff and fold in carefully.

Put in a well-greased soufflé mold, dusted with flour. Put mold in a pan of warm water 3 inches high. Bake at 350° for 1 hour.

Turn out on a round platter and sprinkle generously with grated cheese. In the middle of the mold, put creamed chicken or mushroom sauce (see page 54).

Any vegetable can be substituted for the broccoli in this recipe. It is an excellent lunch dish or side dish to any meat course.

Serves 6

STUFFED GREEN PEPPER
(Toltott Paprika)

3 tablespoons rice
6 green peppers
1 medium-sized onion, finely chopped
2 tablespoons butter, melted
1 pound ground meat
1 egg
salt and pepper to taste
2-1/2 cups tomato sauce (see page 54)

Simmer rice in 5 tablespoons water for 10 minutes.

Cut off the top of the peppers at the stem and scoop out seeds. Sauté onion in butter until transparent. Remove from pan and combine with meat, rice, egg, salt, and pepper. Fill green peppers with meat mixture. Bring tomato sauce to a boil, add peppers and simmer well covered 1 hour or until peppers are tender.

Variation: Cut peppers crosswise and fill. Place on a baking dish. Add 2 cups of beef broth to the dish and bake at 350° for 45 to 50 minutes.

Serve peppers with sautéed mushrooms and potatoes.

Serves 6

Vegetables

GREEN PEAS
(Zold Borso Fozelek)

2 pounds fresh peas, or
   1 10-ounce package frozen peas
1/4 cup hot water
1/2 teaspoon salt
1 teaspoon sugar
1-1/2 tablespoons finely chopped parsley
2 tablespoons butter
2 tablespoons all-purpose flour
1 cup chicken broth

Boil peas 10 minutes in a covered saucepan with the water, salt, and sugar. Add parsley and butter and simmer slowly until peas are tender. Sprinkle with flour and add chicken broth. Stir constantly until thick.

Serves 4 to 6

STUFFED TOMATO
(Toltott Paradicsom)

8 medium-sized, firm tomatoes
1/2 pound ham, or leftover meat, minced
2 hard-boiled eggs, finely chopped
1/2 cup sour cream
chopped parsley to taste
salt and pepper to taste
8 teaspoons grated Parmesan cheese

Cut the tops off the tomatoes and carefully scoop out the seeds and pulp; save pulp. Mix meat, eggs, half the sour cream, parsley, salt, and pepper. Stuff tomatoes with mixture. Cook tops and pulp of the tomatoes and put through a sieve or purée in a blender; put in a flat baking dish. Place stuffed tomatoes on top of the puréed tomatoes and sprinkle with the remaining sour cream, salt, and grated cheese. Bake at 375° 15 to 20 minutes.

This is very good as a side dish or even as a first course.

Serves 6 to 8

SERBIAN GOULASH
(Lecso)

5 large, thick green peppers
4 tomatoes
4 tablespoons bacon drippings
1 onion, finely chopped
1-1/2 teaspoons Hungarian paprika
salt to taste

Core the green peppers and cut into rings. Dip the tomatoes briefly in boiling water; peel and slice them. Sauté onion in bacon drippings until transparent. Add paprika, green peppers, tomatoes, and salt. Simmer covered until pepper is tender.

This is a very good side dish. If sausage is added to the goulash, it may be served for lunch with steamed potatoes on the side. This is another dish from southern Hungary and plays a very important part in Hungarian cooking.

Serves 6

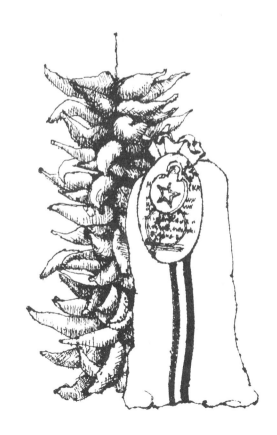

Vegetables

STUFFED KOHLRABI
(Toltott Kalarabe)

6 kohlrabi
3 tablespoons butter
1 tablespoon finely chopped parsley
1/2 pound ground beef
1 egg
1 slice bread, soaked in milk
salt and pepper to taste
1 green onion, finely chopped
2 tablespoons all-purpose flour
1/2 cup sour cream
2 slices cheddar cheese for garnish

Peel kohlrabi and cut off bottoms. Shred the tender leaves and set aside. Wash kohlrabi and scoop out the insides and set aside. Put butter on the bottom of a baking dish, along with the kohlrabi insides, leaves, and parsley.

Prepare filling by combining meat, egg, bread, salt, pepper, and green onion. Place in scooped out kohlrabi. If there is leftover filling, make small meatballs and place on top of the kohlrabi leaves, along with the stuffed kohlrabi. Cover with 1/2 cup water and simmer, covered, until kohlrabi is tender. If needed, add more water gradually.

Combine flour and sour cream. Remove filled kohlrabi and meatballs from the pan and add sour cream mixture to the kohlrabi leaves and insides. Transfer to a baking dish, putting meatballs and stuffed kohlrabi on top. Put a little square of the cheese on each meatball. Keep warm in the oven at 300° until ready to serve. The cheese looks nice and gives the meatballs a better taste.

Vegetables

MIXED VEGETABLE PLATTER
(Vegyes Fozelek Tal)

1 small head cauliflower, whole
1 pound fresh green beans
1 pound carrots, cut lengthwise
1 10-ounce package frozen, small peas
1 pound asparagus
2 medium-sized potatoes
salt and sugar to taste
4 tablespoons butter
1/2 cup sour cream
2 tablespoons bread crumbs
2 tablespoons grated cheese
1/4 cup slivered almonds, sautéed

Cook each vegetable separately with a little salt and a dash of sugar—don't overcook. Make French-fried potatoes (see page 76). Keep vegetables warm on the top of the stove.

Put cooked cauliflower on a large ovenproof platter and pour sour cream over the middle. Sprinkle with bread crumbs and cheese and top with a pat of butter. Bake at 375° 20 to 25 minutes or until golden. Drain all vegetables and pour melted butter over the top. Arrange around the cauliflower in a pinwheel, alternating colors; sprinkle with almonds. Serve immediately.

This is acknowledged as one of the most elegant dishes on European menus. Many people order it in restaurants as a main course. The price is almost as high as a meat dish.

Serves 8 to 10

RICE EXCELLENT
(Remek Rizs)

1/4 pound butter
1 pound fresh mushrooms, sliced
3 tablespoons finely chopped green onions
3 cups diced celery
1/4 cup finely chopped parsley
1/2 cup slivered almonds
2 cups rice (white and wild mixed)
4 cups chicken broth
1/2 teaspoon marjoram (optional)
1/2 teaspoon basil (optional)
salt and pepper to taste

Melt butter in a large frying pan. Add mushrooms, onion, celery, parsley, and almonds and simmer for 1 hour. Meanwhile, cook rice in chicken broth. Add marjoram and basil to rice, if desired.

Combine cooked rice and vegetables. Salt and pepper to taste. Let stand well covered for 1 to 2 hours to take on the delicate flavors. If you serve rice, it should be excellent.

Serves 6 to 8

BROWNED POTATOES
(Resztelt Krumpli)

4 to 5 medium-sized potatoes
1 onion, finely chopped
3 tablespoons butter, melted
salt to taste

Boil potatoes in skins. When tender peel and cut into small cubes. Sauté onion in butter until golden. Add potatoes and salt and mix well. Cook 10 to 15 minutes, turning occasionally. The potatoes should be kept warm on a low flame to take on the onion flavor.

This is a very good side dish for any roast or meat served with gravy or sauce.

Serves 6

RICE SUPERB
(Felseges Rizs)

1 cup raw rice
1 8-ounce can onion soup
1 cup water
1/2 cup slivered almonds
1/4 pound butter

Combine all ingredients, holding out some almonds for garnish. Put in a baking dish, cover, and bake at 350° for 1 hour.
Variation: If it complements the main course, add 1/4 pound mushrooms, sliced.

Serves 6

Vegetables

FRENCH-FRIED POTATOES
(Szalma Burgonya Rohscheiben)

4 medium-sized potatoes
vegetable oil for deep frying
salt to taste

Peel and wash potatoes. Wipe dry and slice very thin. Deep fry in hot oil until golden. Oil should be at least 3 inches deep. Salt and serve immediately.

If necessary, the potatoes can be kept in a warm oven on a baking sheet lined with paper towels. Don't salt, however, until ready to serve.

I cannot make enough of these for my grandchildren. They tell me that my "granny chips" are better than the store-bought variety.

Serves 4 to 6

LAYER POTATOES IN CASSEROLE
(Lerakott Krumpli)

6 to 8 Idaho potatoes
4 to 5 hard-boiled eggs
salt and pepper to taste
1 pint sour cream
1/2 pound ground ham
1/4 pound butter
3 tablespoons grated Parmesan cheese
Hungarian paprika

Boil the potatoes in their skins until tender. Cool, peel, and cut into thin, round slices.

Butter an oven casserole. Arrange a layer of potatoes on the bottom, then a layer of egg slices. Sprinkle with salt and pepper then spread with sour cream. Add some of the ground ham and dot with pieces of butter. Continue alternating the layers, ending with potatoes. Top with the remaining sour cream and sprinkle with Parmesan cheese, salt, and paprika and dots of butter. Bake at 375° for 30 to 40 minutes.

One can vary this casserole by omitting the ham.

Serves 6 to 8

POTATO CROQUETTES
(Krumpli Krokett)

1 pound potatoes
1 tablespoon butter
2 eggs
1-3/4 cups all-purpose flour
1 tablespoon cream of wheat
1/4 cup grated Parmesan cheese
1 tablespoon finely chopped parsley
1 teaspoon salt
vegetable oil for deep frying

Coating
1 to 2 eggs
1/2 cup all-purpose flour
1/2 cup bread crumbs

Boil potatoes in their skins until tender; peel and put through a potato ricer. Cool and put in a bowl, along with the butter, eggs, flour, cream of wheat, cheese, parsley, and salt. Knead into an elastic dough.

Turn out on a floured board and shape into carrot forms with your hand. Roll in flour, dip in egg, and roll in bread crumbs. Deep fry in oil.

This is a very fancy side dish for any meat served with gravy. Put a sprig of parsley on the tip of each croquette to make the impression of a real carrot.

Serves 6

PAPRIKA POTATOES
(OR POOR MAN'S GOULASH)
(Paprikas Krumpli)

1 onion, chopped
3 tablespoons butter or bacon drippings
1 tablespoon Hungarian paprika
6 medium-sized potatoes, peeled and diced
1/2 green pepper, sliced
1/2 tomato, sliced
salt to taste
1 cup water
sausage or hot dogs (optional)

Sauté the onion in butter or in bacon drippings until transparent. Add paprika, potatoes, green pepper, tomato, salt, and water. Simmer 30 to 40 minutes or until potatoes are tender; don't stir, but shake pan occasionally. Sausage or hot dogs may be added the last 10 minutes.

Serves 6

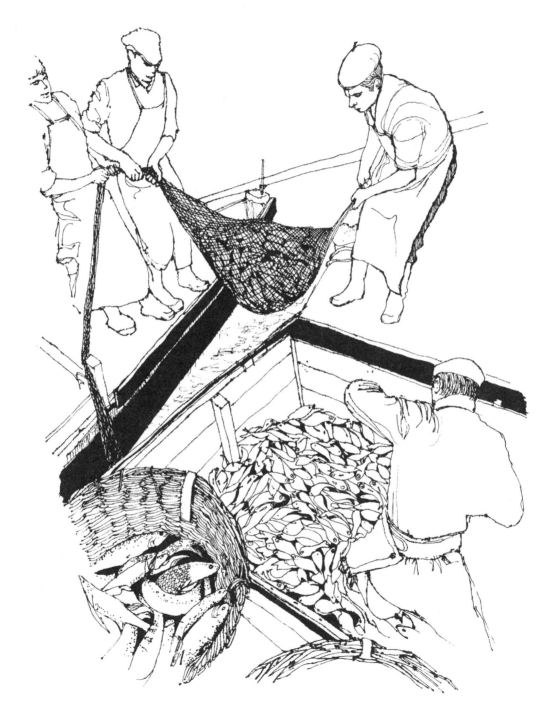

Meat, Poultry and Fish

As the Magyars were historically nomads, wandering through the great plains with their herds, meat was their primary food. The Magyars' herds of cattle were also important as beasts of labor to pull and plow taking some of the load off the people.

From this time originates a cooking kettle called *bogracs*. It was used by the open fire to prepare goulash *(gulyas)* and *tarhonya,* a dried dough easily carried (now known as egg barley).

The Magyars also dried thinly sliced beef in the sun and cooked it with the barley. This tasted something like beef jerky.

Next to beef, pork is the most popular meat in Hungary. Veal is a real delicacy, as it must be very young and milk-fed so that the meat is tender and light colored.

Meat, Poultry and Fish

Lamb is traditionally served at Easter. It is also young, milk-fed and one of the most delicately flavorful of the meats. When the lamb is older, it is highly seasoned and also very enjoyable. Such a dish is found most often in the country.

Chicken is well known as a special Sunday meal. Hungarian cookery has many ways of preparing the young spring chickens. To show how highly chicken is valued, it is often said that "in Hungary when a peasant kills a chicken, either the chicken or the peasant must be sick."

Duck and goose livers are famous in Hungary and are almost always on the menus of fine restaurants. The ducks and geese are fattened with corn so that they become extra large and can provide cooking fat year round. In my pantry were many crocks filled with the ducks and geese stored in their own fat for later use.

Turkey is served on very rare and festive occasions, usually at Christmas. It is most often stuffed with chestnut dressing.

Fish is ample in Hungary, provided by two big rivers—the Danube and the Tisza—and by Lake Balaton. The most excellent fish are the fogas and the sullo. These fish are well known in Europe, as they are exported from Hungary to many countries. They have a tender, mild, snow-white flesh without many bones and are of incomparable quality. Hungary also has trout, sturgeon, pike, and carp—all fresh-water fish.

It took a long time for me to find the right fish in America to adapt to my Hungarian recipes. Even though they are good, they don't taste like the fish of the old times in the old country.

LEG OF VEAL
(Sult Borjucomb)

3 to 4 pound leg of veal, veal shoulder,
   or rib with kidney
salt and pepper to taste
3 to 4 slices bacon
1 onion, sliced
2 cloves garlic, sliced
1 green pepper, sliced
1 tomato, sliced
3 tablespoons butter, melted
Hungarian paprika to taste
white wine to taste

Wash meat and dry with a paper towel. Season with salt and pepper. Place bacon slices in the bottom of a roasting pan and put seasoned meat on top. Add onion, garlic, green pepper, and tomato. Pour butter over the top and sprinkle with paprika.

It is very practical to use the new, see-through, plastic roasting wrap. This seals in all the juices of the vegetables with the meat.

Cover and roast at 375° for 1 to 1-1/2 hours. Check tenderness. If the meat seems dry, pour several tablespoons of wine over it. Increase the oven temperature to 450° and continue baking uncovered until the meat turns golden brown and is completely tender.

This delicious roast should be carved at the table. Strain gravy, mashing the cooked vegetables up with it, and serve on the side.

Serves 6 to 8

VEAL PAPRIKA
(Borju Porkolt)

2 pounds veal stew meat or boneless shoulder
1 large onion, chopped
3 tablespoons butter
1-1/2 tablespoons Hungarian paprika
1 green pepper, sliced
1 tomato, sliced
1 teaspoon salt
water as needed
green pepper rings and tomato slices

Wash and cut meat into 1-inch cubes. Sauté onion in a heavy skillet in the fat until transparent. Remove from heat and add paprika, green pepper, tomato, meat, and salt. Cover skillet tightly and simmer over medium heat, stirring occasionally and adding small amounts of water as needed. Simmer 45 to 60 minutes or until tender. Serve with spatzle (see page 106).

Place meat on a warm platter, leaving room on one side for the noodles, and pour the paprika sauce from the pan over the meat. Garnish with green pepper rings and tomato slices. If possible, serve on preheated plates.

Serves 4

Meat, Poultry and Fish

VEAL FRICASSEE
(Becsinalt Borju)

2 pounds veal shoulder or stew meat
1 teaspoon salt
4 cups water
3 to 4 carrots, sliced
2 stalks celery, sliced
3 tablespoons chopped parsley
1 green onion, whole
2 tablespoons butter
2 tablespoons all-purpose flour
6 to 8 medium-sized mushrooms, sliced
1/2 teaspoon black pepper
1 pound green peas

Cut the meat in 1-inch cubes and put in a kettle with 4 cups salted water. Bring to a boil, skim off foam with a slotted spoon, and reduce heat. Add carrots, celery, 1 tablespoon of the parsley, and the green onion. Simmer 40 to 45 minutes or until meat and vegetables are tender; remove onion.

Melt butter in a skillet, stir in flour and let bubble until lightly browned. Add to meat and vegetables along with the mushrooms, remaining parsley, and black pepper. If necessary, add more water.

Simmer 5 minutes, add green peas and cook until tender. The vegetables used in this dish can be varied to your own taste. Cauliflower and asparagus are both good substitutes, or serve the vegetables separately. Lemon juice may also be added. Serve with steamed rice or steamed potatoes.

Serves 4 to 6

VEAL TURNOVERS
(Gombas Borju Szelet)

2 to 2-1/2 pounds veal steak
salt and pepper to taste
1/2 pound mushrooms
1/4 pound butter
3 tablespoons chopped parsley
1/2 onion, chopped
1 to 2 tablespoons white wine
1/2 cup chicken broth
3/4 cup sour cream
2 tablespoons all-purpose flour

Pound veal steaks and cut in even pieces about 4 to 4-1/2 inches round. Salt lightly. Slice half of the mushrooms and set aside. Chop and sauté the remaining mushrooms in 1 tablespoon butter, salt, and pepper. Place 1 tablespoon of the sautéed mushrooms in the middle of each veal steak and fold meat over; fasten with toothpicks on 3 sides.

Melt remaining butter in a skillet and brown the meat turnovers several minutes per side. Add parsley, onion, wine, and chicken broth; simmer slowly 30 to 40 minutes or until tender.

Transfer meat to a baking dish. Mix sour cream and flour and add to the pan gravy, along with the sliced mushrooms. Simmer for 2 to 3 minutes and pour over meat. Keep in the oven until serving time.

This dish is very good served with potato croquettes (page 77) or with buttered noodles.

Serves 4 to 6

Meat, Poultry and Fish

WIENER SCHNITZEL
(Becsi Szelet)

6 veal cutlets, or 2 pounds veal steak
salt and pepper to taste
1 cup all-purpose flour
2 eggs, well beaten
1 cup bread crumbs
vegetable oil for deep frying
lemon slices and parsley for garnish

Pound meat well, nicking edges with the point of the knife to keep them from curling. Season lightly with salt and pepper. Dip both sides first in flour, then in eggs, and finally in bread crumbs. Slowly fry in a large skillet in deep, hot oil. Leave the lid on when frying the first side, then remove and fry the second side until crisp. Garnish with lemon slices and parsley. With potatoes, salad, and green peas, this makes a real gourmet meal.

Natur schnitzel (Natur szelet): Omit eggs and bread crumbs. Sauté cutlets in 4 tablespoons butter 4 to 5 minutes on each side or until golden brown. Remove to a platter and add 1/2 cup water to the meat drippings. Cook several minutes stirring constantly and pour over the schnitzel.

Parisian schnitzel (Parisi szelet): Omit bread crumb coating.

Serves 4 to 6

VEAL STEAKS WITH HAM AND CHEESE SAUCE
(Sonkas Sajtos Borju Szelet)

Wiener schnitzel, preceding
4 tablespoons butter
3 tablespoons all-purpose flour
2 cups milk
1 egg
1 cup chopped ham
1/2 teaspoon white pepper
1/2 cup grated cheddar cheese
butter

Prepare veal steaks according to Wiener schnitzel recipe. Make white sauce by melting butter in a saucepan. Add flour and when mixture bubbles add milk, stirring constantly. Simmer over low heat 5 to 6 minutes.

Cool and add egg, ham, pepper, and half of the cheese. Pour half of the sauce in a large baking dish, arrange veal steaks on top, and add remaining sauce. Be sure the meat is well covered and sprinkle with the remaining cheese. Dot with little pieces of butter and bake at 350° for 30 minutes or until golden.

This is a very tasty, elegant meal with potato croquettes (see page 77) as a side dish.

Serves 4 to 6

Meat, Poultry and Fish

STUFFED VEAL BREAST
(Toltott Borju Mell)

3 to 4 pound veal breast
4 to 5 green onions, chopped
3/4 cup butter
8 slices white bread, soaked in water or milk
1 teaspoon salt
1/4 teaspoon pepper
3 tablespoons finely chopped parsley
4 to 5 mushrooms, chopped
6 eggs, well beaten
Hungarian paprika to taste
1/4 cup water or white wine

Have the butcher make a pocket in the veal breast. Wash in cold water, rinse, and wipe dry.

Sauté green onion in 1/2 cup butter until lightly browned. Squeeze liquid from the bread and add, along with salt, pepper, parsley, and mushrooms, stirring constantly until warm. Add eggs; continue stirring constantly until eggs are set.

Stuff the veal pocket with mixture and sew closed, or fasten with skewers to prevent the stuffing from leaking out.

Place the stuffed breast in a large baking pan. Melt the remaining butter and pour over the roast; sprinkle with paprika. Cover and roast at 350° for 1-1/2 to 2 hours, basting often. Uncover and sprinkle with water or white wine. Increase oven temperature to 400° and continue cooking and basting for 1 hour, or until golden brown and tender.

Remove roast to a warm platter, taking out string or skewers. Let stand 10 to 15 minutes and carve 1/2-inch thick with a sharp knife. Keep warm and serve with gravy in a gravy boat.

Serves 6 to 8

SWEET AND SOUR BEEF
(Pacolt Marhahus)

Marinade
1 cup wine vinegar
1 cup dry red wine
2 to 3 bay leaves
6 to 8 peppercorns
1 onion, sliced
2 carrots, sliced

3 to 4 pound boneless pot, rump,
　　chuck, or round roast
salt and pepper to taste
3 tablespoons all-purpose flour
1/4 cup bacon drippings
3 carrots, sliced
3 medium-sized onions, sliced
1 tablespoon sugar
3/4 cup sour cream
2 tablespoons raisins
2 tablespoons capers

Combine marinade ingredients. Place meat seasoned with salt and pepper in marinade, cover, and refrigerate for 3 days. Turn meat in the marinade each day. On the third day, drain the meat, reserving the marinade. Dry meat well and rub with 2 tablespoons flour. Brown in bacon drippings on all sides. Add carrots, onions, 2 cups of the marinade, and the sugar. Cover and cook over low heat for 2 hours or until tender, turning several times and adding more marinade as liquid dissolves.

Put meat on a cutting board, cool, and slice. Place on a large, ovenproof platter. Strain pan gravy. Combine sour cream and 1 tablespoon flour and stir into the strained gravy. Add raisins and capers. Add more sugar or marinade to taste. Simmer gravy for 2 to 3 minutes and pour over sliced meat. Cover with foil and keep warm in the oven at a low temperature until ready to serve.

It is a must that this meat be served in its own gravy with some kind of dumplings on the side. Bread or bacon dumplings are the most popular with this dish.

Serves 6 to 8

Meat, Poultry and Fish

BEEF BIRDS ROULADE
(Gongyolt Szelet)

2 pounds round steak, sliced
salt and pepper to taste
3 slices bacon, cut in 1-inch pieces
1/2 pound mushrooms, chopped
1 to 2 green onions, chopped
2 teaspoons chopped parsley
2 to 3 eggs, well beaten
1 teaspoon capers, chopped
3 tablespoons shortening
1 green pepper slice

Pound meat into even, thin slices so that they look nice when served. Sprinkle salt and pepper on both sides. Brown bacon in a skillet and add mushrooms, onion, and parsley and brown for 2 to 3 minutes. Add well-beaten eggs and stir constantly until set. Remove pan from heat and add capers and more salt if needed. Spread mixture evenly on meat slices, roll up, and fasten with toothpicks or skewers. If you are using larger slices, roll up lengthwise and tie with a cord; slice before serving.

Heat fat in a skillet and add meat roulades; slowly brown on all sides. Gradually add hot water to cover bottom of the pan, cover, and simmer 2 hours or until meat is tender when pierced with a fork. When tender put roulades on a serving platter, cover, and keep warm in the oven until ready to serve.

Make pan gravy by scraping the sides of the skillet, adding green pepper, and 1 cup water. Boil briskly stirring constantly until liquid is reduced by one-half. Taste, add seasoning if necessary, and pour over meat.

Variations: The mushrooms can be replaced with ham or a strip of pickle can be added down the middle of each roulade. You can also replace the gravy water with beef broth or wine.

This dish is perfect with one of my rice recipes.

Serves 4 to 6

HUNGARIAN POT ROAST WITH POTATOES
(Parolt Marha Hus Burgonyaval)

2 to 3 pound chuck roast
salt, pepper, and 1 teaspoon flour
4 tablespoons bacon drippings
2 onions, finely chopped
3 cloves garlic, finely chopped
1 tomato, sliced
1 green pepper, sliced
1 to 2 bay leaves
2 tablespoons minced parsley
4 potatoes
green pepper rings

Dredge the meat in flour, salt, and pepper mixture. Sear both sides of the meat in the bacon drippings. Add onion, garlic, tomato, green pepper, bay leaves, parsley, and 1 cup water. Simmer on top of the stove or bake at 300° for 2 to 3 hours or until tender. Turn meat occasionally so that it will cook evenly; if necessary, add more water.

When meat is tender remove to an ovenproof platter and keep covered in the oven at a low temperature. Meanwhile, make pan gravy by straining meat juices. Peel potatoes and slice lengthwise into 1/2-inch pieces. Place in the gravy, along with the meat and 1-1/2 cups water. Simmer 20 to 30 minutes or until potatoes are tender.

Slice meat thin, diagonally across the grain. Place on heated platter, pour hot gravy over, put potatoes on side. Garnish with pepper rings.

Serves 4 to 6

Meat, Poultry and Fish

SKILLET STEAK
(Serpenyos Rostelyos)

2 to 2-1/2 pounds round steak
1/4 cup bacon drippings
2 onions, sliced
1 tablespoon Hungarian paprika
1/2 green pepper, sliced in rings

Cut meat into serving-size pieces and pound. Brown meat and onions in bacon drippings. Sprinkle paprika over meat and add pepper rings. Cover and simmer on very low heat for 1-1/2 to 2 hours or until tender. Turn several times so that the meat is not overbrowned, adding a few spoonfuls of water each time.

This steak can be prepared a day ahead and warmed up when ready to serve. Egg barley and vegetables go well with the steak.

Serves 4 to 6

PEPPER AND GARLIC STEAK
(Borsos, Fokhagymas Marha Szelet)

1-1/2 to 2 pounds beef sirloin or
   Jewish filet, cut in thin slices
1 tablespoon salt
1 teaspoon black pepper
3 slices bacon
3 cloves garlic, finely chopped
1 tablespoon chopped parsley

Pound meat slices, nicking edges with the point of the knife to keep them from curling. Rub with salt and pepper. Brown bacon and reserve. Add meat to bacon drippings and brown. Add garlic and 1/2 cup water. Cover tightly and simmer slowly until tender, adding more water when necessary. Put parsley over meat and cook an additional 4 to 5 minutes. Serve hot, garnished with the crumbled bacon.

This steak is very good with mashed potatoes.

Serves 4

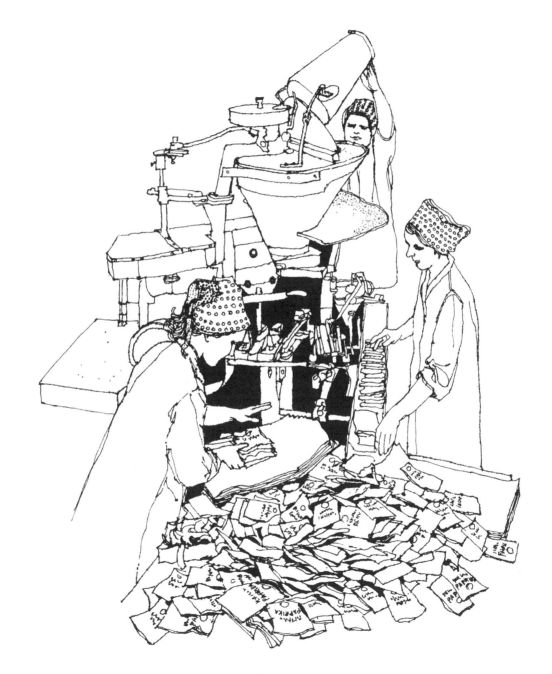

Meat, Poultry and Fish

CHICKEN BREAST À LA BUDAPEST
(Pesti Csirke)

5 whole chicken breasts
1/4 pound butter
salt and pepper to taste
4 to 5 green onions, chopped
3 to 4 cloves garlic, sliced
1/2 pint sour cream
1 teaspoon Worcestershire sauce
2 tablespoons bread crumbs
1 teaspoon Hungarian paprika
1/2 cup dry, white wine
parsley for garnish

Cut each chicken breast in half lengthwise. Remove skin and larger bones. Rinse and pat dry with a paper towel.

Melt butter in a long baking dish. Place the chicken pieces on the bottom flesh side down. Sprinkle with salt and pepper, turn, and sprinkle the other side. Arrange side by side; divide onion and garlic evenly and place between or under the chicken pieces. Combine the sour cream with the Worcestershire sauce and a little salt and pepper and pour over the chicken so that it is completely covered. Sprinkle the top with bread crumbs and paprika.

Bake at 375° for 1-1/2 hours. After 30 minutes, add half of the wine, pouring it on the side. Bake another 20 minutes and add remaining wine. Garnish with parsley. You will be surprised at the excellent combination of flavors in this dish.

Serves 6 to 8

Hint: Save the chicken bones until you have enough to make a soup stock. Save the skin in the freezer to make crackling. This is a good, crisp appetizer.

Crackling: Put chicken skin in a pot, add 1 cup water and simmer slowly until all the water evaporates, stirring occasionally. This lets all the fat out, leaving the skin crisp. Put cracklings on a paper towel and sprinkle with salt and paprika. Save the fat remaining in the pan in a jar for cooking.

STUFFED CHICKEN
(Toltott Csirke)

Stuffing
4 green onions, chopped
3/4 cup butter
6 slices white bread, soaked in milk or water
1 teaspoon salt
1/4 teaspoon pepper
2 tablespoons chopped parsley
3 to 4 mushrooms, chopped
1 chicken liver, chopped
5 eggs, well beaten

1-1/2 to 2 pound chicken
1 tablespoon salt
Hungarian paprika

Sauté green onions in 1/2 cup melted butter until lightly browned. Squeeze liquid out of the bread and add to the green onion, along with salt, pepper, parsley, mushrooms, and liver. Add eggs and stir constantly until eggs are set. Cool.

Prepare chicken for stuffing by washing insides and outsides well; dry with paper towel and sprinkle with salt. Carefully lift skin over the breast with your finger, beginning at the neck. Continue separating skin from flesh with your finger, going over the breast, thighs and legs. Spread stuffing evenly between the skin and flesh, molding stuffing so that chicken holds its shape. Make sure that skin is pulled well over the stuffing so that it will not come out during baking. Put remaining stuffing in the chicken cavity.

Place the stuffed chicken in a baking pan. Melt remaining butter and pour over the chicken; sprinkle lightly with paprika.

Cover and bake at 350° for 1 to 1-1/2 hours, or 25 minutes per pound. Baste several times while cooking and remove lid the last 45 minutes so that top will brown.

It is not necessary to use skewers to keep the filling inside. This stuffing will not overflow. The main thing is to see that the eggs are well set when making the stuffing.

Variation: Turkey The same stuffing can be used for turkey, adding cooked, peeled, cubed chestnuts. Do not stuff turkey as described for chicken; rather put some stuffing under the neck and in the stomach cavity. If a large turkey is being stuffed, double the filling recipe. I know from experience that this is so tasty you cannot have too much.

Serves 4

Meat, Poultry and Fish

CHICKEN BIRDS
(Csirke Tekercsek)

6 to 8 chicken breasts, halved and boned
6 to 8 slices dry beef or thin slices of ham
6 to 8 slices bacon
1 10-1/2-ounce can mushroom soup
1/2 cup sour cream
parsley and tomato slices

Wrap each piece of chicken breast in a ham slice; wrap a piece of bacon around the outside. Put side by side in a baking dish. Combine mushroom soup and sour cream and pour over. Bake at 275° for 3 to 4 hours. Don't add any salt.

Garnish with parsley and tomato slices and serve with peas and carrots. If desired, pour the gravy into an extra bowl and serve on the side. This is very tasty!

The chicken birds can be prepared for baking the day before.

Serves 4 to 6

PAPRIKA CHICKEN
(Paprikas Csirke)

1 large onion, sliced in rings
4 tablespoons butter
1-1/2 tablespoons Hungarian paprika
1-1/2 pound chicken, washed, cut up, and salted
1 green pepper, sliced
1 tomato, sliced
1/4 pound mushrooms (optional)
1/2 cup sour cream (optional)

Sauté onion rings in butter in a 3-quart pot or Dutch oven until transparent. Remove from heat and add paprika, chicken, half of the green pepper, and half of the tomato. Cover tightly with a lid and simmer slowly for 1-1/2 hours. Occasionally turn pieces over so they will cook evenly. If necessary, add small amounts of water. If mushrooms are used, add during last 15 minutes of cooking time.

When meat is tender, transfer to a baking dish. Make pan gravy, scraping onion from the pan and adding a little water. Pour over chicken. Garnish with remaining green pepper and tomato. Cover with foil and keep warm in the oven at a low temperature until ready to serve. Sour cream can be added to the gravy, but that is up to the individual's taste. You must try both ways. Spatzle is the usual side dish but buttered noodles goes very well with this dish, too.

Serves 4

PORK ROAST
(Diszno Sult)

3 to 4 pound pork loin, rib shoulder, or leg
1 large sausage
4 slices bacon
1 large onion, sliced
4 cloves garlic, sliced
1/2 green pepper, sliced
2 teaspoons caraway seeds
1 cup water

Ask your butcher to remove the larger bones from the roast and to make little cuts in the remaining bones for easier carving. He must also put the sausage lengthwise through the middle of the meat. (The sausage should be the same length as the roast.)

Rub roast with salt, pepper and herbs of your choice. Cut crisscross slits along the fat side of the meat. Put bacon slices in the bottom of a roasting pan with a tight-fitting lid. Add the roast, onion, garlic, green pepper, caraway seeds, and water.

Roast covered at 350° for 2 hours or until tender (pork needs about 45 minutes per pound). Baste meat frequently. Uncover and increase heat to 400° the last half hour. Before serving, raise heat to 500° for several minutes to get a crisp roast.

Transfer to serving platter. Strain pan gravy and serve on the side in a gravy boat. This roast is also good cold and sliced very thin on a buffet.

Serves 6 to 8

PORK CHOPS WITH SAUERKRAUT
(Kaposztas Sertesborda)

6 to 8 pork chops
1/4 cup bacon drippings
1 onion, chopped
1-1/2 teaspoons Hungarian paprika
1 16-ounce can sauerkraut,
    strained (reserving liquid)
1 cup water
1/2 green pepper, sliced in rings
1/2 pint sour cream
green pepper rings for garnish

Pound pork chops and lightly salt; then brown them in their own fat. Sauté onion in bacon drippings until transparent. Add paprika, sauerkraut, and water; simmer 2 to 3 minutes. Place pork chops and green pepper rings on the sauerkraut and simmer 1 hour. Before serving add sour cream and some of the sauerkraut liquid (if tartness is desired). Garnish with green pepper rings.

Serves 6

Meat, Poultry and Fish

FRIED SWEETBREADS
(Rantott Mirigy)

2 quarts water
1 tablespoon salt
juice of 1/2 lemon
1/2 onion
2 pounds veal or beef sweetbreads
2 tablespoons salt
3/4 cup all-purpose flour
2 to 3 eggs, well beaten
3/4 cup bread crumbs
vegetable oil for deep frying
parsley and lemon slices for garnish

Boil water with salt, lemon juice, and onion. Add sweetbreads and simmer 30 to 35 minutes (beef requires more cooking time than veal). Strain and rinse several times.

Cool and peel off skin and membrane. Cut lengthwise once or twice to get nice, flat slices. Lightly salt and coat with flour. Dip in egg and then in bread crumbs. Deep fry in hot oil at least 3 inches deep on a medium-high flame.

Remove to paper towel and keep warm in the oven at a low temperature until ready to serve. Garnish with parsley and lemon slices. You can also serve with cold pickle sauce (see page 53) for a fine delicacy.

Serves 4 to 6

SWEETBREADS IN MUSHROOM SAUCE
(Mirigy Gombaval)

8 cups water
1 tablespoon salt
juice of 1/2 lemon
2 pounds veal or beef sweetbreads
3 tablespoons chopped green onions
2 tablespoons butter
2 tablespoons all-purpose flour
1/2 pound mushrooms, halved or quartered
2 tablespoons chopped parsley
2 cups chicken broth
salt and pepper to taste
grated cheddar cheese to taste
fresh parsley sprig for garnish

Boil water with salt and lemon juice. Add sweetbreads, cover, and simmer 25 to 30 minutes (beef requires more cooking time than veal). Strain and rinse several times. Cool and peel off skin and membranes. Cut sweetbreads into 2-inch cubes.

Make mushroom sauce by sautéing green onions in butter, stirring constantly until transparent. Add flour, mushrooms, and parsley and brown 2 to 3 minutes. Add chicken broth and bring to a boil. Reduce heat and add sweetbreads, salt, and pepper. Simmer 5 to 10 minutes.

Pour into a baking dish and sprinkle with grated cheese. Keep warm in the oven at a low temperature until ready to serve.

Garnish with a fresh sprig of parsley.

Serves 4 to 6

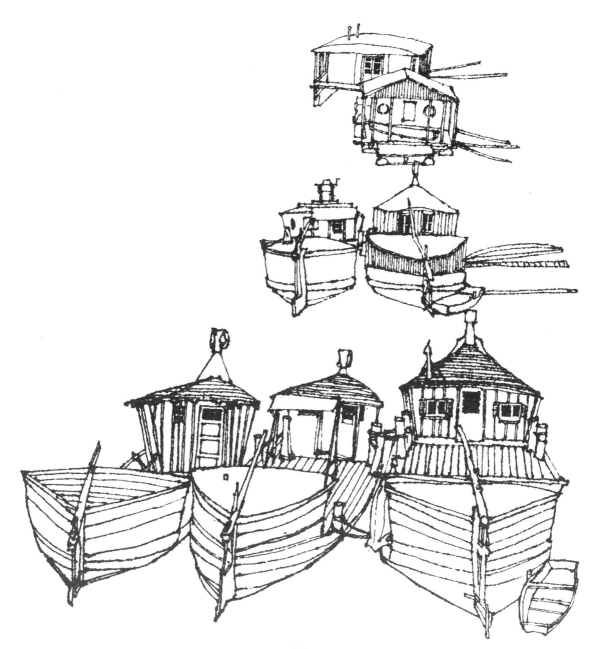

Meat, Poultry and Fish

FISH À LA GYPSY
(Ciganyos Hal)

4 medium-sized potatoes
2 pounds fish filet (pike, trout, or sole)
2 green peppers, sliced
2 tomatoes, sliced
1 small onion, sliced
5 tablespoons sour cream
3 tablespoons half-and-half
2/3 cup butter
salt, pepper, and Hungarian paprika to taste

Cook potatoes in skin until almost tender. Peel and cut into thick slices. Cover the bottom of a well-buttered baking dish with the potatoes. Sprinkle salt on the potatoes to taste.

Place fish filets over potato slices and cover with the green pepper, tomatoes, and onion. Combine sour cream and half-and-half and spoon over the top. Sprinkle with salt, pepper, and paprika.

Bake 10 minutes at 425° and baste with its own juice. Lower temperature to 300° and bake 25 to 30 minutes or until fish is tender and the top is nice and golden.

Serves 6

FISH IN NUT SAUCE
(Dios Hal)

2 carrots
1 stalk celery
3 sprigs parsley
4 to 5 peppercorns
salt and pepper to taste
4 cups water
2 pounds halibut steak
2 tablespoons all-purpose flour
1/2 cup chopped walnuts
parsley for garnish

Put carrots, celery, parsley, peppercorns, salt and water in a kettle. Cover and simmer 25 minutes. Strain liquid into a shallow pan, reserving 2 tablespoons for sauce. Bring to a boil and place fish pieces in the stock. Simmer 5 to 6 minutes or until fish is white and flaky. Combine flour with the reserved stock. Add to the simmering fish, along with the nuts. Cook on a low flame 5 to 6 minutes. Season with a little fresh ground pepper and salt, if needed.

Garnish with fresh parsley and serve hot with steamed potatoes.

Serves 4 to 6

FISHERMAN'S SOUP
(Halaszle)

2 to 3 pounds assorted fresh-water fish
2 teaspoons salt
2 to 3 large onions, sliced
1-1/2 tablespoons Hungarian paprika
1 tomato, sliced
1 green pepper, sliced

The key to a real good fish soup is to use different kinds of fish such as trout, pike, bass, and halibut. Wash and bone fish, saving heads and bones; cut into 2-inch pieces and salt. Put the fish bones and heads and onions into a saucepan; cover with water and bring to a boil. When the water begins to boil, add paprika. Simmer on a low flame for 1 hour. Strain fish stock and put the salted fish pieces in a kettle with the stock, tomato, and green pepper. Simmer uncovered for 20 to 25 minutes. Don't stir the soup but just shake the pan from time to time while cooking. This will prevent the fish from breaking.

Remove fish from the kettle with a slotted spoon and put in a large serving bowl; strain broth over the fish. Serve hot.

Jellied: Add 1 envelope unflavored gelatin to every 2 cups liquid. Dissolve gelatin in 1 cup hot soup. Return to kettle and stir. Brush a mold with fine oil, add soup and chill. This must be prepared a day ahead. Garnish with cherry tomatoes and hard-boiled eggs and serve on shredded lettuce.

This is good when dinner is served buffet style, or as the first course of a large dinner, or for a complete lunch.
Serves 4 to 6

Hungarian fishermen can still be found on the river banks of Duna, Tisza and Lake Balaton, cooking this heavenly soup in big kettles on an open fire. They use lots of small fish to make a rich stock. (Small fish are good only for soup stock because they have so many little bones.) While the soup is cooking the fishermen shake the kettle, preventing the fish from breaking.

The restaurants in Hungary that serve fish dishes are called *Halasz csarda* (fish wayside inn).

Meat, Poultry and Fish

AGI'S FAVORITE FISH POTPOURRI
(Agi Kedvenc Hal Kevereke)

1/2 cup dry vermouth
3 green onions, finely chopped
4 tablespoons butter
2 to 3 pounds filet of sole
3/4 cup sliced mushrooms
3/4 cup small cooked shrimp
1 10-1/2-ounce can cream of shrimp soup
1/2 pint cream
4 to 5 tablespoons all-purpose flour
3/4 cup grated cheese, half Parmesan and
    half Swiss
salt and pepper

Put vermouth, onion, and butter (holding out a small part of the onion and butter) in a pan with a tight-fitting lid; let simmer. Cut filet of sole lengthwise and roll up, securing with a toothpick. Add to the pan and poach covered for 2 to 3 minutes or until the inside is a light, pink color. Carefully remove fish and take out toothpicks. Put in a buttered baking dish. Sauté mushrooms with remaining onions and butter and put around fish rolls, along with the shrimp.

Make sauce by adding the shrimp soup to the liquid in the pan. Mix cream and flour until smooth and add to the pan, along with half of the grated cheese. Heat and stir until sauce thickens. Season to taste with salt and pepper. Pour sauce over fish rolls, mushrooms, and shrimp in the baking dish. Sprinkle with remaining cheese.

Put in a 350° oven for 25 to 30 minutes. Remove and put under the broiler until golden. Serve with boiled or steamed parsley potatoes.

This dish can be prepared ahead and baked the day of serving. This is my daughter Agi's favorite recipe as it is very fast to prepare and yet has an excellent result. She sometimes uses crab as well; the more variety of fish, the more flavor.

Serves 6

FISH ROLLS IN EGG SAUCE
(Gongyolt Hal Tojas Sauceban)

1-1/2 pounds filet of sole
salt and pepper to taste
1-1/2 tablespoons lemon juice
1/2 cup boiling water, or dry vermouth
2 carrots, peeled and sliced
2 slices onion
leaves from 2 stalks celery
2 tablespoons butter
2 tablespoons all-purpose flour
1/3 cup heavy cream or milk
3 hard-boiled eggs, separated
1 pound asparagus, cooked

Sprinkle fish filets with salt, pepper, and lemon juice. Roll up and secure with toothpicks.

Put water or vermouth in a large frying pan and bring to a boil; add carrots, onion, and celery leaves. Cover and simmer 5 minutes. Add fish rolls, cover and simmer another 5 minutes.

Put fish rolls on an ovenproof platter and remove toothpicks. Strain cooking liquid and save. Put butter in a saucepan, melt, and add flour, stirring until lightly browned. Add strained liquid and cream. Simmer and stir until it comes to a boil. Season to taste, adding chopped egg whites. Arrange asparagus beside fish rolls, cover with sauce, and garnish with grated egg yolks.

Serves 4

FISH IN DILL SAUCE
(Kapros Hal)

2 pounds filet of sole
salt, pepper, and flour to taste
4 tablespoons butter
1/2 pint sour cream
1/2 cup beer
fresh dill weed to taste

Sprinkle fish filet with salt, pepper and flour. Melt butter in a shallow pan and fry fish on both sides until golden. Remove carefully with a spatula to an ovenproof dish.

Mix sour cream with beer and pour over fish to cover. Sprinkle generously with dill. Keep warm in the oven at a low temperature until ready to serve. Before serving, put under the broiler for 2 to 3 minutes. Sprinkle a little more dill on the top and serve immediately.

Serves 4 to 6

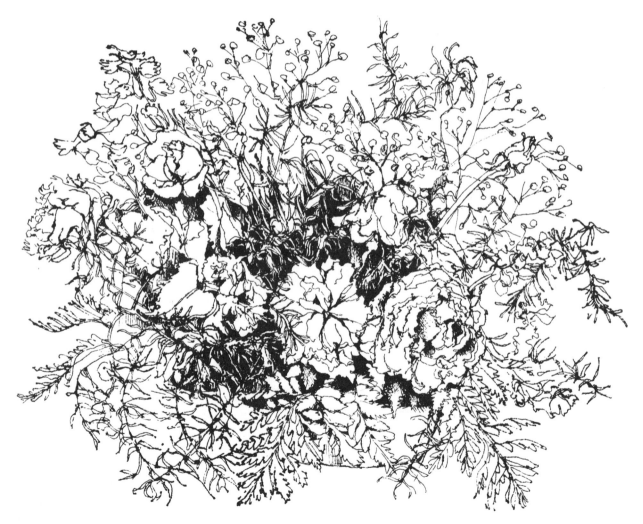

Noodles, Pancakes and Dumplings

Perhaps no country has such a large variety of side dishes as Hungary. Many of these can also be served as a main course or entrée, or even as a fancy dessert for special dinners. As you will see in the following recipes, one can make miracles from basic ingredients: flour, eggs, water, and milk.

Boiled pastry noodles play a great part in Hungarian meals. They were once always prepared from scratch with flour, eggs, and water; today excellent ready-made noodles can be substituted at times. Hungarian noodles are so variable they can serve as soup garnishes, side dishes to meats, casserole or main dishes, and even as desserts.

Hungarian pancakes have a long history and are now universally popular. The art of making these pancakes, crêpes, or *palacsinta*, takes some practice. The most important thing to learn is how to swirl the pan with the batter quickly enough to get evenly rounded, thin, delicate pancakes. They are fried one by one and there is no limit to the many ways they can be used. They can be rolled, folded, or layered and filled with a favorite spread. They can be served warm or made in advance and frozen until ready to use and warmed in the oven. One can even make an impressive, flaming dessert.

Dumplings can also be widely varied. If you choose well and present them with imagination, even the biggest potato eater will favor them for their wonderful taste.

Noodles, Pancakes and Dumplings

BASIC NOODLES
(Gyurt Teszta)

2 cups sifted, all-purpose flour
1 teaspoon salt
2 eggs, well beaten
3 to 5 tablespoons water
2 quarts salted water
4 tablespoons butter, melted

Put flour in a bowl and make a well in the center. Add salt, eggs, and enough water to make the dough stiff.

Turn dough onto a floured board and knead into a smooth, shiny ball; cover with a towel and let stand for 10 minutes.

Roll dough about 1/8-inch thick; if sticking, sprinkle underneath with flour. Continue rolling by turning over dough; let dry 5 minutes.

Cut dough into 3-inch-long noodles. Stack up, sprinkling flour between each. When almost ready to serve, drop noodles into boiling water. When they rise to the surface, rinse with cold water and drain. Put in a serving dish and pour melted butter over the noodles.

These noodles can be used as a soup garnish, a side dish to any meat with gravy, or as an entrée.

In my well-equipped pantry in Hungary, all different shapes of cut noodles hung in cloth bags. My maids prepared the noodles in the summer when eggs were plentiful.

Serves 6

In America we can replace the homemade noodles with a variety of excellent, ready-made, egg noodles. Use a 1-pound package of noodles and cook in salted water until tender. Put in a colander, rinse, and drain well. Place in a casserole dish and pour melted butter over. Stir noodles with a fork.

NOODLE VARIATIONS

With walnuts (dios metelt): Mix together 1/3 cup powdered sugar, 1 cup finely chopped walnuts, and 1 teaspoon grated orange rind. Top each serving of cooked noodles with this mixture.

With poppy seeds (makos metelt): Mix together 1 can Solo poppy-seed mixture, 1 teaspoon vanilla, and 1 teaspoon grated lemon rind. Top each serving of cooked noodles with this mixture.

With cottage cheese (turos csusza): Top each serving of cooked noodles with cottage cheese and sour cream. Sprinkle with cooked, crumbled bacon *or* generously dust with powdered sugar.

With chopped meat (vagdalt hus toltelek): Brown 1/2 pound ground meat in 1 tablespoon butter with salt, pepper, and parsley to taste. When cooked add 2 well-beaten eggs. Alternate layers of noodles with layers of the ground meat and grated cheese. Put noodles on the top and cover with 1/2 cup sour cream and a little grated cheese. Bake at 350° for 30 to 35 minutes.

With ground ham (sonkas metelt): Combine 1/2 pound ground or chopped ham, 1/4 cup sour cream, 2 eggs, and pepper to taste. Put noodles and ham mixture in a buttered baking dish. Top with 1/4 cup sour cream and sprinkle with Parmesan cheese. Bake at 350° for 30 to 35 minutes. These meat-filled noodles go well with a green salad.

With cabbage (kaposztas kocka): Fry 1 small, shredded cabbage in 4 tablespoons butter with 1 teaspoon sugar, salt, and pepper to taste until lightly golden, stirring constantly. Cover and let stand 10 minutes. Mix noodles thoroughly with cabbage and serve hot as a side dish.

Layered noodle casserole (lerakott metelt): Put a layer of cooked noodles in a buttered baking dish. Mix together 1/2 cup chopped walnuts and 1/4 cup sugar and put on top of the noodles, holding out a small amount for garnish. Put another layer of noodles in the casserole and top with 3 tablespoons of jam. Add another layer of noodles to the casserole and top with 2 squares of grated, sweet chocolate. Add another layer of noodles and sprinkle with powdered sugar and the remaining nut mixture. Bake at 350° for 30 to 35 minutes.

If you want a very elegant dessert, top the noodles with meringue and sprinkle with powdered sugar and nuts before putting in the oven.

Noodles, Pancakes and Dumplings

SPATZLE
(Nokedli)

2-1/2 cups all-purpose flour
3 teaspoons salt
1 tablespoon cream of wheat
2 eggs
9 cups water
5 tablespoons butter, melted

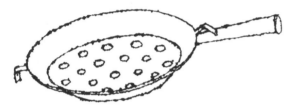

Put flour, 1 teaspoon salt, and cream of wheat in a bowl. Make a well in the middle and add eggs, 1 cup water, and 1 tablespoon butter; stir well until batter is smooth and thick.

Turn batter onto a cheese board and cut into almond-sized pieces, dropping into 8 cups of boiling water with 2 teaspoons salt. Cook only half of the batter at one time to avoid crowding. Stir the bottom of the pot with a wooden spoon so that the dumplings will rise to the surface. After dumplings rise, cook gently 1 to 2 minutes. Remove from water with a slotted spoon, toss lightly with 4 tablespoons butter, and put in a serving dish.

In Europe there is a colander-type utensil with holes larger than a cherry stone. Portions of the dough can be put in this colander over the boiling water and forced through with a spoon. This allows the dough to drop more evenly and faster into the water. Until I brought one of these colanders from Europe, I used a lid to a bacon fryer that had big holes in it. If you must use a cutting board, hold it over the boiling water in your left hand and cut pieces off with a knife, dropping them into the boiling water. It is important that the water boil all the time and your knife be dipped in the water after each dumpling is cut.

Serves 4 to 6

STYRIAI NOODLES
(Styriai Metelt)

2 to 2-1/4 cups all-purpose flour
1 pound baker's cheese
6 eggs
1/2 teaspoon salt
3/4 to 1 cup sugar
1/2 pint sour cream
1 teaspoon grated lemon rind
4 tablespoons butter
1 tablespoon vanilla
1/3 cup raisins
powdered sugar for garnish

Put flour and baker's cheese in a bowl and make a well in the center. Add 1 whole egg and 1 egg yolk, salt, 1 tablespoon sugar and 1 tablespoon sour cream. Mix into a dough—not too stiff.

Turn dough onto a lightly floured board, divide into 2 or 3 parts and shape into rounds. Roll out 1/4 to 1/2 inch thick and cut lengthwise into 3-inch strips. Stack on top of each other, sprinkling flour between each.

Drop noodles into boiling salted water and stir occasionally with a fork. When noodles rise to the surface, strain and rinse in cold water. Cream together egg yolks, lemon rind, remaining sugar, butter, vanilla, and sour cream. Fold in 5 well-beaten, stiff egg whites and raisins. Combine noodles and egg mixture and pour into a buttered baking dish. Bake at 350° for 30 to 35 minutes. Serve warm sprinkled with powdered sugar.

These are my daughter's favorite noodles. It took me a long time to discover baker's cheese which is the right replacement for our European cottage cheese.

This is the best of all the noodles so it is worth preparing your own dough.

Serves 6

Noodles, Pancakes and Dumplings

EGG BARLEY
(Tarhonya)

1 cup egg barley
2 tablespoons butter, melted
1/2 small onion, finely chopped
salt and pepper to taste
1 bouillon cube
1 tablespoon finely chopped parsley
2 cups boiling water

Brown barley in butter in a pan. When golden, add onion and stir constantly 2 to 3 minutes. Mix salt, pepper, bouillon cube, and parsley with boiling water and pour over barley. Cover tightly and simmer on a slow flame, or put in a 350° oven, for 30 minutes. If all the liquid is absorbed before barley is tender, add more water—not too much so that it doesn't get soaked.

Serve with stew or with meat that has a paprika gravy. I could give the basic recipe for making *tarhonya* from scratch, but I don't think anybody would want such a big job when Manischewitz provides us with good, ready-made barley.

This is one of the old-time, dried foods that the Magyars took along on their wanderings. The dough was made from flour, egg, and enough water to prepare a very stiff dough. They cut the dough in small pieces and dried it in the sun. In my pantry, barley that had been dried in the summer sun was hanging in a cloth bag.

Serves 4 to 6

SPINACH NOODLE SOUFFLÉ
(Spenot Soufflé)

1 pound package of noodles
4 tablespoons butter
3 to 4 green onions, minced
2 bunches spinach, cooked, drained, and chopped
1 10-1/2-ounce can cheddar cheese soup
1 pint sour cream
2 eggs
salt, pepper, and garlic salt to taste
grated cheddar or Parmesan cheese for garnish

Cook noodles in boiling water with 1 teaspoon salt; don't overcook. Drain well. Melt butter in a skillet and add onions, stirring until limp. Remove from fire and add spinach, cheddar cheese soup, sour cream, eggs, salt, pepper, and garlic salt to taste; toss noodles in this mixture.

Put in a buttered baking dish and sprinkle with grated cheese. Bake at 375° for 35 minutes.

This can be prepared a day before baking. I always double the portion because this is one of my family's favorites.

Serves 6

Noodles, Pancakes and Dumplings

CHEESE MACARONI
(Sajtos Makaroni)

1-1/2 cups elbow macaroni
1 medium-sized onion, finely chopped
4 quarts salted water
2 tablespoons butter
1 tablespoon all-purpose flour
1 cup cold milk
2 eggs
1/2 pound medium-sharp cheddar cheese, grated

Cook macaroni and onion in boiling salted water for 15 minutes.

Meanwhile prepare white sauce. Melt butter in a saucepan; add flour and stir until mixture bubbles. Add milk and stir until the sauce thickens; remove from flame and stir constantly until smooth. When cool stir in whole eggs.

Butter a baking dish and put in half of the macaroni. Sprinkle with 2/3 of the grated cheese and add the remaining macaroni. Pour sauce over the top and sprinkle with remaining cheese. Bake at 375° for 30 to 35 minutes.

Serves 6

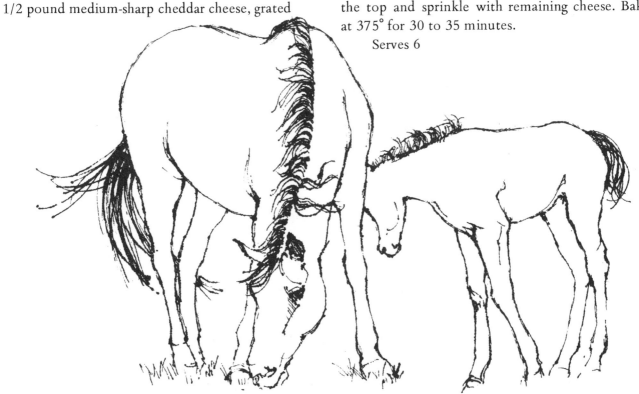

PANCAKES FOR APPETIZERS
(Palacsinta Mint Eloetel)

2-1/4 cups sifted, all-purpose flour
3 eggs
2 cups milk
2 tablespoons butter, melted
2 tablespoons cognac
dash salt
melted butter for frying
grated Parmesan cheese

Combine flour, eggs, and milk. Add butter, cognac, and salt. Cover well and let batter stand for 3 hours or overnight in the refrigerator.

Heat a 3-1/2x3-1/2-inch crêpe pan until moderately hot; lightly butter. Remove pan from heat and pour in just enough batter to cover the bottom of the pan. Immediately tilt pan back and forth to spread batter thinly and evenly. Fry pancake over medium heat until golden. Loosen edges with a spatula, turn pancake, and fry second side. Repeat with remainder of batter, buttering pan lightly each time. If batter thickens on standing, stir in a small amount of additional milk.

Fill each pancake with chosen filling and roll up, tucking in ends well. Place side by side in a baking dish. Brush with melted butter and sprinkle with grated Parmesan cheese. Brown at 375° for 20 minutes. Put a toothpick in each pancake and serve. This can be prepared a day ahead; brown just before serving.

Serves 6

PANCAKE FILLINGS

Meat: Grind 1/2 pound cooked beef or chopped ham and 1 small, minced onion; combine with a few drops of Worcestershire sauce, pepper, salt, and enough sour cream to make a thick mixture.

Cheese: Mix 1/2 cup cream cheese and 1/2 cup grated cheddar cheese. Season with a little dill, pepper, a few drops of Worcestershire sauce, 1/4 teaspoon prepared mustard, and salt. If the filling needs moistening, add a little sour cream.

Mushroom: Sauté 1/2 pound mushrooms, washed and minced, with a small minced onion in 4 tablespoons butter; do not let brown. Add 2 to 4 tablespoons heavy cream and continue to sauté until all the liquid has been absorbed. Pour in 2 well-beaten eggs and stir until creamy. Season with Hungarian paprika, salt, white pepper, and plenty of minced parsley.

Egg: Hard boil 3 or 4 eggs; shell and put through a fine sieve. Mix in 1/4 teaspoon anchovy paste, 1/4 teaspoon white pepper, 1/4 teaspoon prepared mustard, and 1 tablespoon heavy cream.

Noodles, Pancakes and Dumplings

FILLED PANCAKES FOR LUNCH
(Toltott Palacsinta Lunchre)

1 cup sifted, all-purpose flour
1 cup milk
1 cup water
1/4 cup butter, melted
4 eggs, slightly beaten
melted butter for frying

For a dessert pancake, add:
1-1/2 tablespoons sugar
1 teaspoon vanilla
1 teaspoon cognac

Put flour in a bowl and make a well in the center. Add milk, water, butter, and eggs. Beat until smooth. Let stand for 2 to 3 hours or overnight in the refrigerator.

Heat a 7x7-inch crêpe pan until moderately hot; lightly butter. Remove pan from heat and pour in 2 to 2-1/2 tablespoons batter, or just enough to cover bottom of pan. Immediately tilt pan back and forth to spread batter thinly and evenly. Fry pancake over medium heat until lightly golden on bottom. Loosen edges with a spatula, turn pancake, and fry on second side. Repeat with remaining batter, buttering pan lightly each time. If batter thickens on standing, stir in a small amount of additional milk.

Fill each pancake with chosen filling and roll or fold up. Put in a buttered baking dish and cover first with waxed paper and then with foil. This recipe can be prepared a day ahead. Reheat at 150° when ready to serve.

Serves 6

PANCAKE FILLINGS

Basic: Melt 4 tablespoons butter in a saucepan and stir in 1/4 cup unsifted flour. Stir until well blended and mixture bubbles (do not let brown). Remove from heat and gradually stir in 2 cups milk. Cook stirring constantly until mixture is thick and smooth. Add salt, pepper, and 2 hard-boiled eggs, chopped. Add 1/2 cup shredded cheese and stir until cheese is melted.

Ham: Add 3/4 cup chopped ham and 1/4 cup chopped black olives to the basic filling.

Spinach: Add 1 cup cooked, well-drained, chopped spinach to the basic filling.

Dessert: Combine 2 egg yolks with 6 tablespoons sugar and 1 teaspoon vanilla and beat; add 1 pound baker's cheese. Beat 2 egg whites until stiff; add 2 tablespoons sugar and add to the baker's cheese mixture, along with 1/4 cup raisins.

Jam: Put 1 to 2 tablespoons jam on each pancake and sprinkle with 1 tablespoon grated nuts.

Chocolate: Mix grated chocolate with equal amounts of grated nuts; or pour hot milk over grated nuts, making a thick paste, and add grated chocolate or cocoa. If cocoa is used, it is necessary to add sugar to taste.

PANCAKE SOUFFLÉ
(Palacsinta Felfujt)

pancakes for lunch (see page 112)
2 cups cooked chopped paprika chicken (see
    page 94) or veal paprika (see page 81) with gravy
1/2 pint sour cream
1/2 cup grated Parmesan cheese

    Cut pancakes into 1/2-inch strips, like noodles. Combine chicken, sour cream, gravy, and half of the cheese. Add to the pancake noodles, holding back 1/4 cup gravy to pour over the top. Sprinkle with remaining grated cheese and serve in a baking dish.

    This is a favorite Hungarian dish. The recipe can be prepared a day ahead, put in a casserole, and refrigerated. Bake at 350° for 45 minutes.

Variation: Substitute 1 cup ground cooked ham for the chicken or veal. Combine 4 egg yolks, sour cream, and ham; fold in well-beaten, stiff egg whites and pancake strips. Put in a buttered double boiler, cover, and steam for 1 hour over boiling water. When ready to serve, turn onto a platter and sprinkle with grated cheese.

    Serves 6

Noodles, Pancakes and Dumplings

CRÊPE FROM THE GREAT PLAIN
(Hortobagyi Palacsinta)

Pancakes
4 eggs
1 cup milk
1 cup water
1 cup flour
4 tablespoons butter, melted
melted butter for frying

Filling
cooked paprika chicken and gravy, including
    mushrooms, sliced (see page 94)
2 hard-boiled eggs, chopped
1 raw egg
2 tablespoons all-purpose flour
1/2 pint sour cream
parsley for garnish

Combine all pancake ingredients and beat with a whisk until smooth. Cover and put in the refrigerator 2 to 3 hours.

Heat a 7x7-inch crêpe pan until moderately hot; lightly butter. Remove pan from heat and pour in 2 to 2-1/2 tablespoons batter, or just enough to cover bottom of pan. Immediately tilt pan back and forth to spread batter thinly and evenly. Fry pancake over medium heat until lightly golden on bottom. Loosen edges with a spatula, turn pancake, and fry on second side. Repeat with remaining batter, buttering pan lightly each time. If batter thickens with standing, stir in a small amount of additional milk.

Debone chicken breasts and legs and cut in small cubes, along with mushrooms. Combine with hard-boiled eggs and the raw egg. Fill pancakes with 2 to 3 tablespoons of the filling. Fold over twice and arrange in a shallow baking dish. Cover and keep warm in the oven.

Combine flour and sour cream and add to the chicken paprika gravy; stir over low heat until gravy thickens. Serve in a gravy boat and pour generously over each portion. Garnish with parsley. These crêpes are perfect for lunch with small green peas and spiced peaches or prunes.

Serves 6

Noodles, Pancakes and Dumplings

PANCAKE HAM ROLL
(Sonkas Tekercs)

Pancakes
1 cup sifted, all-purpose flour
1-1/2 cups milk
1/2 cup water
4 tablespoons butter, melted
2 whole eggs plus 2 yolks, slightly beaten
melted butter for frying
grated Parmesan cheese and parsley sprigs
   for garnish

Filling
1 pound ground ham
1/2 pint sour cream
2 eggs
white pepper to taste

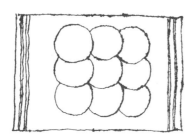

Put flour in a bowl and make a well in the center; add milk, water, butter, and eggs. Make a smooth batter with a whisk. Let stand for several hours in the refrigerator.

Heat a 7x7-inch crêpe pan until moderately hot; lightly butter. Remove pan from heat and pour in just enough batter to cover the bottom of the pan. Immediately tilt pan back and forth to spread batter thinly and evenly. Fry pancake over medium heat until golden. Loosen edges with a spatula, turn pancake, and fry second side. Repeat with remainder of batter, buttering pan lightly each time. If batter thickens on standing, stir in a small amount of additional milk.

Nine pancakes are needed for the ham roll. Put pancakes on a lightly buttered, square-shaped kitchen towel; spread ham filling on top. Roll up like a jelly roll and cover with the towel, tying the ends with a string. Put in a big kettle of boiling, unsalted water for 20 minutes.

Take out of the water and put on a long meat platter; remove kitchen towel and sprinkle ham roll generously with grated Parmesan cheese. Garnish with parsley sprigs. Serve with mushroom sauce (see page 54) on the side. This is a complete lunch or an entrée for a big dinner.

Serves 4 to 6

LAYERED HAM PANCAKES
(Rakott Sonkas Palacsinta)

6 eggs, separated
1-1/3 cups heavy cream
3/4 cup all-purpose flour
4 tablespoons butter, melted
salt to taste
1 pound chopped ham
3/4 cup plus 2 tablespoons sour cream
pepper to taste
1 to 2 tablespoons half-and-half
melted butter for frying

Combine egg yolks, heavy cream, flour, and butter to make pancake batter. Fold in well-beaten, stiff egg whites and salt to taste.

Heat 7x7-inch crêpe pan until moderately hot; lightly butter. Remove pan from heat and pour in 4 to 4-1/2 tablespoons batter, covering bottom of pan. Immediately tilt pan back and forth to spread batter evenly. Pancakes should be about 1/2 inch thick. Fry pancake over medium heat until lightly golden on bottom. Loosen edges with a spatula and remove from pan; brown only one side. Repeat with remaining batter, buttering pan lightly each time. Make 6 or 7 pancakes from the batter.

Combine ham, 2 tablespoons sour cream, and pepper. Place pancakes on top of each other in a baking dish, sprinkling the unbrowned side of each pancake with the ham mixture.

Combine 3/4 cup sour cream and half-and-half and pour over the pancakes. Bake at 400° for 8 to 10 minutes. Cut and serve like a layer cake.

Serves 4 to 6

Noodles, Pancakes and Dumplings

**FANCY PANCAKES WITH
NUT FILLING AND CHOCOLATE SAUCE**
(Dios Palacsinta Csokolade Martassal)

Pancakes
4 eggs
1-1/2 cups sifted, all-purpose flour
2 cups milk
1 teaspoon brandy
1 teaspoon fine oil
pinch of salt
melted sweet butter for frying

Filling
1 cup milk
1-1/2 cups ground walnuts
4 tablespoons sugar
1/4 cup raisins
1 tablespoon grated orange rind
2 tablespoons rum

Sauce
4 squares Baker's semi-sweet chocolate
2 tablespoons sugar
1 tablespoon cocoa
2 egg yolks
1 teaspoon flour
1/4 cup milk
1 tablespoon rum

Combine all ingredients for pancake batter and beat well. Cover and let stand for 1 hour.

Heat a 7x7-inch crêpe pan until moderately hot; lightly butter. Remove pan from heat and pour in 2 to 2-1/2 tablespoons batter, or just enough to cover bottom of pan. Immediately tilt pan back and forth to spread batter thinly and evenly. Fry pancake over medium heat until lightly golden on bottom. Loosen edges with a spatula, turn pancake, and fry on second side. Repeat with remaining batter, buttering pan lightly each time. If batter thickens on standing, stir in a small amount of additional milk.

To make filling bring milk to a boil in a saucepan, mix in ground walnuts, sugar, raisins, and orange rind. Cook for 2 to 3 minutes on very low heat, stirring constantly. Remove from heat and mix in rum. Spread 1 tablespoon of filling on each pancake and roll up. Put in a buttered baking dish and keep warm in the oven at 100° to 150°.

To make sauce put chocolate, sugar, and cocoa in a double boiler and melt until smooth. Beat egg yolks, flour, and milk together; add to melted chocolate. Heat sauce, stirring until it is thick—don't bring to a boil. Add the rum. Immediately pour sauce over each serving of pancakes. (This sauce cannot be reheated.)

This dessert can also be served flaming by adding warm rum and igniting.

This recipe was the specialty of one of the best known Hungarian chefs, Gundel, who presided at two of the best-known restaurants in Budapest, City Park and Hotel Gellert. If you were ordering these pancakes, it was enough to say "I want the specialty of the house."

Serves 6

Noodles, Pancakes and Dumplings

SLIPPED PANCAKES
(Csusztatott Palacsinta)

4 tablespoons butter
5 eggs, separated
1/4 cup sugar
1 teaspoon vanilla
1/4 cup all-purpose flour
1 cup milk
dash of salt
vanilla-flavored powdered sugar to taste
melted butter for frying
sliced almonds

Cream butter with egg yolks and sugar; add vanilla, flour, milk, and salt. Fold in well-beaten, stiff egg whites.

Heat a 7x7-inch crêpe pan until moderately hot; lightly butter. Pour 1/4 cup batter into the skillet, making the pancake thicker than usual. Fry one side on slow heat until golden; do not spread batter or tilt pan.

Slip onto a buttered baking dish and sprinkle vanilla-flavored powdered sugar on the unbrowned side. Put the next pancake on top and repeat the process. If the stack becomes higher than a layer cake before all the batter is used, begin another stack. Put pancake stack in the oven at 300° for 10 to 15 minutes or until top is lightly golden.

Sprinkle top with vanilla-flavored powdered sugar and almonds and serve at once. To serve, cut like a layer cake.

These are one of the best of all pancakes. They are light and flavorful, rich and delicate; and they are good even without a filling.

Variation: Sprinkle powdered sugar and grated chocolate in between pancakes; top with ground walnuts or almonds.

Variation: Cover the top with well-beaten, stiff egg whites to which 1 tablespoon of sugar has been added for each egg. Sprinkle with slivered almonds.
Serves 4

POTATO PANCAKES
(Krumplis Palacsinta)

3 cups grated, raw potatoes
3 eggs
3 tablespoons all-purpose flour
1/2 cup finely chopped onion (optional)
salt and pepper to taste
vegetable oil for frying

Combine all ingredients. Drop a spoonful into the hot oil and flatten with a spoon. Brown both sides until golden and put on paper towel to absorb excess oil. Serve hot and fresh.

Serves 4 to 6

121

Noodles, Pancakes and Dumplings

POTATO DUMPLINGS
(Krumplis Gomboc, Nudli)

4 potatoes, boiled in their skins
1/2 teaspoon salt
2 eggs
1 tablespoon butter
1 cup all-purpose flour
1/4 cup cream of wheat
6 plums with seeds removed and
    replaced with a lump of sugar
1 cup bread crumbs, browned in 1/4 pound butter

Peel potatoes and press through a potato ricer. Cool and put in a bowl, along with the salt, eggs, butter, flour, and cream of wheat. If necessary, add a little more flour so that the dough is easy to work with.

Turn out on a floured board and knead well; form into a large, sausage-shaped roll. Roll dough into 3-inch squares, about 1/4 inch thick. Carefully put a plum in the center of each square and shape into the form of a dumpling; pinching dough together so that it doesn't break in the hot water.

When all dumplings are made, drop into a large pot of boiling water and simmer 5 to 10 minutes on low heat. Carefully remove dumplings one by one with a slotted spoon; roll in bread crumbs.

Variation: Potato Noodles Roll dough into the shape of a small sausage. Cut off noodles 2 inches long. Cook in boiling salted water for 5 to 10 minutes. Drain and roll in bread crumbs.

Variation: Dessert Potato Noodles To serve noodles as a dessert, sprinkle with cinnamon and sugar. These noodles are one of the favorite desserts not only of Hungarians, but of anyone who has tasted them.

BAKER'S CHEESE DUMPLINGS
(Turos Gomboc)

1 pound baker's cheese
3 eggs, separated
pinch of salt
1/4 cup cream of wheat
3/4 cup bread crumbs, browned in
    4 tablespoons butter
1/4 cup all-purpose flour
powdered sugar to taste
1/2 pint sour cream

Mix baker's cheese with egg yolks. Beat egg whites with a pinch of salt until stiff. Fold into egg-yolk mixture alternately with cream of wheat. Let stand for 1 hour.

Shape small dumplings with wet hands and roll in flour. Put in boiling water over a low flame. After dumplings rise to the surface, cook 1 to 2 minutes. Remove with a slotted spoon and roll in bread crumbs until well covered. Sprinkle with powdered sugar and serve immediately with sour cream on the side.

If you must keep the dumplings warm in the oven for a short time, put a few spoonfuls of the sour cream on top. When ready to serve, sprinkle with powdered sugar and serve with remaining sour cream on the side.

Serves 4 to 6

CLARA'S BAKER'S CHEESE DUMPLINGS
(Klara Turos Gomboc)

2 eggs
1 teaspoon salt
1/2 pound baker's cheese
3 to 4 tablespoons bread crumbs
1/2 cup bread crumbs, browned in butter
jam, sour cream, and powdered sugar to taste

Mix eggs, salt, and baker's cheese; add 3 tablespoons bread crumbs. Shape a dumpling and drop into the boiling water. If it holds its shape, add the remaining dumplings; if not, add an additional tablespoon of bread crumbs to the batter. When dumplings rise to the surface, cook 1 to 2 minutes. Remove with a slotted spoon and roll in remaining bread crumbs. Serve with powdered sugar, sour cream, and jam on the side.

Baker's cheese dumplings are so excellent it is worth trying them. It is important that they be light, fluffy, and served warm.

Serves 4

Noodles, Pancakes and Dumplings

BREAD DUMPLINGS
(Zsemle Gomboc)

4 slices white bread, 1 to 2 days old
3 to 4 quarts water plus 1 cup
3 teaspoons salt
2-1/2 cups all-purpose flour
2 tablespoons cream of wheat
2 eggs
1/2 cup plus 1 tablespoon butter, melted

Cut bread into cubes and brown in butter. Bring water and 2 teaspoons salt to boil. Mix flour, cream of wheat, and 1 teaspoon salt; combine with eggs, 1 cup water, and 1 tablespoon melted butter to make a smooth batter. Fold in crisp bread cubes. Cut out dumplings with a spoon and drop into the boiling water.

When dumplings rise to the surface, cook 2 to 3 minutes. Take one out with a slotted spoon and cut in half to test for doneness. If the center is not white or floury, the dumplings are cooked.

Put dumplings in a pan and pour 1/2 cup melted butter over. Keep covered in a warm oven until ready to serve—don't let them dry out.

This is one of the best side dishes for stews, cabbage dishes, or sauerbraten.

Serves 6

BACON DUMPLINGS
(Szalonnas Szalvetas Gomboc)

15 slices stale white bread
1 cup milk
5 slices bacon
5 eggs
salt, pepper, and parsley to taste
2 tablespoons all-purpose flour
1 tablespoon cream of wheat
4 tablespoons butter
grated Parmesan cheese or browned bread crumbs

Cut half of the bread into small cubes; soak remaining bread in milk.

Brown bacon and remove to a paper towel. Sauté cubed bread in bacon fat until crisp and golden. Beat eggs; add salt, pepper, and parsley. Press soaked bread through a sieve and add to eggs, along with bread cubes and crumbled bacon. Let stand for 1 hour.

Add flour and cream of wheat. If dough is too runny, add more flour.

Take a square napkin and brush well with cold butter, pour in dough and tie with a string—it should look like a big ball. Drop into salted boiling water; cover and cook 30 to 45 minutes.

Open napkin and turn out large dumpling on a platter. Sprinkle with browned bread crumbs or Parmesan cheese. Cut like a melon.

This is a fancy version of bread dumplings and is ever so good as a side dish to any meat course.

Serves 6

POTATO DOUGHNUT WITH HAM FILLING
(*Krumplis Fank Sonkaval*)

1 square or envelope yeast
3 tablespoons milk, lukewarm
4 medium-sized potatoes, baked and peeled
4 tablespoons butter, melted
4 egg yolks
1 teaspoon salt
1-1/4 cups all-purpose flour

Filling
1/4 pound chopped ham
1 egg yolk
1 tablespoon sour cream
salt and pepper to taste
vegetable oil for deep frying
grated Parmesan cheese for garnish

Melt yeast in lukewarm milk. Put baked potatoes through a potato ricer and combine with butter, yeast, egg yolks, salt, and flour. Combine all filling ingredients and mix well.

Turn dough onto a floured board and roll about 1/4 inch thick. Cut into 3-inch circles and put a small spoonful of the filling in the center of half of the circles. Cover with remaining circles. Cut filled doughnuts a second time with a smaller-sized cutter so that the edges are well sealed. Cover with a towel and let rise. Deep fry in oil until golden brown; remove and roll in grated Parmesan cheese. Serve immediately.

Serves 4 to 6

Variation: Meat Filling

1 small onion, finely chopped
2 tablespoons butter
1 tablespoon chopped green pepper
1 tablespoon Hungarian paprika
1/2 pound ground beef
salt and pepper to taste
1 egg
1 tablespoon sour cream

This is a glamorized version of Hungarian piroshky!

Sauté onion in butter until golden; add green pepper and stir 1 to 2 minutes. Sprinkle with paprika and immediately add meat, salt, and pepper. Stir well, pour 1/2 cup water over, and simmer covered until all meat is browned and liquid is absorbed. Remove from heat, leaving lid on until completely cool. Mix in egg and sour cream.

This is excellent with cocktails and if you make the doughnuts smaller, they are nice as a finger food.

I can remember when I entertained in my old country how the maids started serving these doughnuts from both ends of the dinner table; or they served them at midnight with refreshments, always piping hot, and made fresh at the last minute.

Serves 4 to 6

126

Breads, Rolls and Coffee Cakes

Hungary is an agricultural country so the harvesting of crops is of great importance. Of the grains, winter wheat is used the most. It is a high-quality, rich flour that is just as good for fine pastries as for bread. The winter wheat is unbleached and glutenous. Rye and corn flour are also used in Hungary.

The harvesters start cutting the wheat at daybreak. Their work must be finished in the shortest time possible, since the ripe heads easily spill the heavy grain in the hot sunshine. During the harvesting of our crops, we sent food to the field in big baskets, wine in big jugs, and always fresh, big, round biscuits *(arato pogacsa)*. When harvesting was over, it was traditional to celebrate with a big festival of dance and music, decorated with wheat garlands. Before the celebration, the villagers took freshly made bread to the church, thanking the Lord for the blessing of the wheat fields.

For villagers, for laborers, and even for city people, the most significant part of their food is homemade bread. Thus Hungarians often compare an excellent person to a choice piece of bread.

Breads, Rolls and Coffee Cakes

BREAD AND LANGOSH
(Kenyer es Langos)

6 cups all-purpose flour
1/2 cup cake flour
1-1/2 packages dry yeast
lukewarm water as needed
1 tablespoon salt
2 potatoes, boiled, peeled, and put through a ricer
2 tablespoons caraway seeds

Sift the flours together and put in a large bowl, making a well in the center. Add yeast and 1 cup lukewarm water, stirring with a wooden spoon until yeast dissolves. Cover with a dish towel and let stand in a warm place for 1/2 hour or until dough bubbles and rises. Add the salt, potatoes, caraway seeds, and water as needed. Mix first with a wooden spoon and then with your hands until you have a moist, slightly sticky dough. Knead until thoroughly mixed and dough is elastic enough to pull away from your hands. Cover and set in a warm place for 1-1/2 to 2 hours or until dough has doubled in bulk.

Turn dough onto a floured board. Knead for at least 10 minutes, pressing the dough down flat and folding it over, until the large air bubbles are squeezed out and the texture is right.

Cut dough into 2 equal sections (or 3 sections if you would like the third part for langosh as a quick taste of the fine dough). Form each of the 2 parts into a smooth log shape and put either in a well-greased bread pan or in a bread pan with a cloth lining. Let dough rise and bake in the pan.

If you want a crisp crust, let dough rise in a bread pan lined with a floured napkin. Turn dough onto a flat cookie sheet and cut diagonal strips along the top with a sharp knife. Lightly smooth the surface with your wet hand.

Bake in a preheated oven at 375° for 45 minutes or until golden. Put on a rack to cool, smooth surface with your wet hand, and cover until bread cools.

Variation: Rye flour can be substituted in this recipe, omitting the potatoes.
Serves 6 to 8

Langosh
Take the third part of the dough and form into round balls. Roll balls into finger-thin, flat 5-inch circles (this is very similar to pizza) and prick with a fork. Fry in a little fat or butter on both sides until golden. (This is the city version of langosh, since we don't have country stoves.)

In Hungary we had our own, special brick oven in the country in which was made fresh-baked langosh for breakfast. The bread dough was flattened into circles, baked, and spread with fresh butter. Oh! I can't forget the wonderful smell and the delicious taste of this fresh-baked bread. In the city, bread was baked once a week in big loaves with a good, crisp crust.
Serves 4

CROISSANTS
(Kifli)

4 cups sifted, all-purpose flour
1-1/2 squares yeast
1/2 teaspoon sugar
lukewarm milk as needed
1 teaspoon salt
3/4 cup butter, melted
1 egg yolk
1 egg, well beaten, plus 1 teaspoon sugar

Put flour in a large bowl and make a well in the center. Add yeast, sugar, and 1/2 cup milk; mix well until yeast dissolves. Cover with a dish towel and let stand in a warm place for 25 to 30 minutes, or until dough bubbles and rises. Add salt, 4 tablespoons butter, egg yolk, and enough milk to make an elastic dough. Knead well until smooth and shiny. Cover and let rise again in a warm place for 1 to 1-1/2 hours or until dough doubles in bulk.

Turn dough onto a floured board and divide into 4 balls. Roll each ball into a circle and brush with the remaining butter. Cut each circle into 8 pie-shaped pieces and roll up into croissants, beginning at the wide end. Put rolls on a baking sheet several inches apart and brush with the egg and sugar mixture. Let stand 15 to 20 minutes and brush again. (If you prefer, sprinkle with poppy or caraway seeds and salt.) Bake in a 375° oven that has been preheated to 400° for 25 to 30 minutes or until golden.

Serves 6

Breads, Rolls and Coffee Cakes

EGG TWIST
(Fonott, Foszlos Kalacs)

4 cups sifted, all-purpose flour
1 square yeast, or 1 package dry yeast
1 cup milk, lukewarm
1/2 cup sugar
1 teaspoon salt
3 egg yolks
3/4 cup butter, melted
1 egg, well beaten

Put flour in a large bowl and make a well in the center. Add yeast, 1/4 cup milk, and 1 tablespoon sugar; mix well until yeast dissolves. Cover with a kitchen towel and put in a warm place for 10 to 15 minutes or until dough bubbles and rises. Combine remaining milk, salt, egg yolks, and 1/4 cup sugar. Add to the bowl and beat with a wooden spoon until dough is smooth and elastic. Gradually stir in 3 tablespoons of the butter, beating well after each tablespoon. Cover and put in a warm place and let dough rise about an hour or until double in bulk.

Turn onto a floured board and divide dough into two parts. Flatten dough into rectangular shapes with palms of hands. Brush with remaining butter; sprinkle with remaining sugar and roll up.

Stretch two rolls by twisting the ends in opposite directions. To braid, lay one strip horizontally on the center of the board and lay the other strip vertically on top, crossing at the center. Take an end of the horizontal strip in each hand and cross over the center strip; repeat until dough is braided.

Put dough on a greased cookie sheet, tucking the ends under. Brush with the beaten egg and let rise for 30 minutes. Brush again with egg and bake in a preheated oven at 350° for 40 to 50 minutes or until golden.

Almost all raised coffee cakes are better torn apart rather than sliced. If you want that excellent homemade taste, serve oven fresh.

Serves 6

ROLLS
(Zsemle)

4 cups sifted, all-purpose flour
1-1/2 squares yeast, or 1-1/2 packages dry yeast
lukewarm milk as needed
4 tablespoons butter, melted and cooled
1/2 teaspoon salt
1 egg, well beaten

Put flour in a large bowl and make a well in the center. Add yeast and 1/2 cup milk; mix well until yeast dissolves. Cover with a dish towel and let stand in a warm place for 30 minutes or until dough bubbles and rises. Add enough milk to make an elastic (not too firm) dough. Mix well with a wooden spoon or with your hand. Add butter and salt and knead well. Cover and let stand in a warm place for 1 to 2 hours or until dough doubles.

Turn onto a lightly floured board and form into balls (the size depends on how big you want your rolls). Put balls on a baking sheet and brush with egg; let stand for 15 to 20 minutes. Brush once more. Preheat oven to 375°; then reduce heat to 350° and bake for 15 to 25 minutes or until golden. Remove rolls from oven and keep covered until ready to serve.

If you want to cut slits in the top of your rolls before baking, they become the emperor's roll, *Csaszar zsemle.* These rolls were named during the Hungarian-Austrian monarchy when the Austrians referred to the king as "emperor."

Serves 6 to 8

BRIOCHE *(Brios)*

2-1/4 cups sifted, all-purpose flour
1 square yeast
1 tablespoon sugar
lukewarm milk as needed
3 egg yolks
6 tablespoons butter, melted and cooled
1 egg, well beaten

Put flour in a large bowl and make a well in the center. Add yeast, sugar, and 1/2 cup milk; mix well until yeast dissolves. Cover with a kitchen towel and put in a warm place for 20 to 25 minutes or until dough bubbles and rises. Add the egg yolks, butter, and enough milk to make an elastic dough. Work dough with a wooden spoon until very smooth and shiny. Cover and let dough rise in a warm place for 1 to 1-1/2 hours or until it doubles in bulk.

Using a teaspoon, take out dough the size of an egg and shape into round balls. Place on a baking sheet several inches apart. Brush with egg and let stand 15 to 20 minutes. Brush again and bake in a 375° oven that has been preheated to 400° for 20 to 25 minutes or until golden.

Serves 4 to 6

Breads, Rolls and Coffee Cakes

RAISED KUGELHUPF
(Kelt Kuglof)

6 cups sifted, all-purpose flour
2 cakes yeast, crumbled, or 2 packages dry yeast
1/2 cup sugar
2 cups milk, lukewarm
4 egg yolks
2 tablespoons sour cream
1/2 teaspoon salt
1/4 pound butter, melted and cooled
1 egg, well beaten
vanilla-flavored powdered sugar or
    chocolate frosting (see page 171) for topping

Filling
2 tablespoons butter, melted
1/4 cup white raisins
4 tablespoons sugar
2 teaspoons vanilla or
    1 tablespoon cinnamon or
    2 to 3 tablespoons cocoa

Put flour in a large bowl and make a well in the center. Add yeast and 1/4 cup sugar; pour 3/4 cup milk over the top. Mix well until yeast is dissolved. Cover with a dish towel and let stand in a warm place for 10 to 15 minutes or until dough bubbles and rises.

Add egg yolks one by one. Combine remaining sugar and milk, sour cream, and salt. Beat into flour with a wooden spoon; continue beating until the dough blisters and leaves spoon clean, gradually adding the butter. Cover dough and set aside in a warm place for 1 hour or until dough doubles.

If filling is not used, add 1/4 cup raisins, 1 teaspoon vanilla, and 1 teaspoon grated lemon rind before kneading dough.

When dough has risen, turn onto a floured board and knead well with your hands. Roll out about 1-1/2 inches thick and spread filling on the top; roll up like a jelly roll.

Put in a well-buttered kugelhupf form, or in a tube pan. The pan should be about half full. Set aside and let dough rise 15 minutes. Brush the top with the beaten egg.

Bake in an oven preheated at 450° for 10 to 15 minutes. Then cover with a heavy brown paper so that the top does not become too brown, and bake an hour at 325°.

Sprinkle with vanilla-flavored powdered sugar or cool and ice.

The kugelhupf pan is also called a "Turk's head"—so named when the Turks ruled Hungary.

Serves 6 to 8

RAISED SWIRLS
(Kelt Csiga)

kugelhupf recipe, preceding
1/2 pound butter
1-1/2 cups sugar
2 cups milk
2 tablespoons vanilla

Prepare recipe for kugelhupf. When dough has risen, turn onto a floured board and knead well with your hands. Cream together butter and 1 cup sugar. Roll out dough 1/2 inch thick and spread with the butter and sugar mixture. Roll up like a jelly roll. If you don't have a big enough pastry board, cut the dough into 2 or 3 sections and make several rolls, dividing the filling between them.

Cut rolled up dough into 1- to 1-1/2-inch slices and put in a well-buttered baking dish several inches apart. Cover and put in a warm place and let dough rise about an hour or until double in bulk.

Bake in a preheated oven at 350° for 10 to 15 minutes or until swirls begin to turn golden. If swirls are to be served immediately, combine milk, 1/2 cup sugar, and vanilla and baste swirls several times until they have turned golden brown. If rolls are to be frozen before using, remove from oven; don't baste until ready to reheat and serve.

These swirls are excellent served oven fresh with coffee.

Serves 6 to 8

Breads, Rolls and Coffee Cakes

MIXED KUGELHUPF COFFEE CAKE
(Kevert Kuglof)

5 eggs, separated
3/4 to 1 cup sugar
1 tablespoon lemon juice
1 teaspoon vanilla
3/4 cup all-purpose flour
1/4 pound butter, melted and cooled
1/4 cup raisins
vanilla-flavored powdered sugar, or
    chocolate frosting (see page 171) for topping

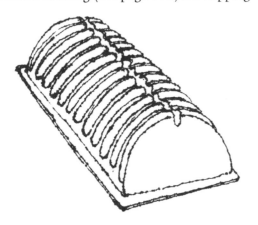

Beat egg whites until stiff; gradually add 1/3 of the sugar and mix until fluffy and rises to a peak. Beat egg yolks, remaining sugar, lemon juice, and vanilla until thick and yellow. Carefully fold in egg whites alternately with flour. Gently fold in butter and raisins.

Pour into a medium-sized, well-buttered and floured kugelhupf form or Bundt pan. Bake in a preheated oven at 350° for 15 minutes; turn heat down to 300° and bake for another 35 to 45 minutes. Test doneness with a needle or a toothpick. Cool on a cookie rack and turn onto a platter. Sprinkle generously with vanilla-flavored powdered sugar or cool and ice.

Variation: Bishop's Bread Bake the same mixture in a deerback form (a rounded loaf pan), adding mixed, cut-up, dried fruit rather than raisins. This is very good with ice cream or on a mixed cookie platter. Serve sliced and nicely arranged. This is the European version of fruit cake.

Serves 6

GOLDEN COFFEE CAKE
(Arany Galuska)

kugelhupf recipe (see page 132)
1 cup sugar
3/4 cup finely chopped walnuts
1-1/2 teaspoons cinnamon
1/4 pound butter, melted
1/2 cup raisins

Prepare kugelhupf recipe. Combine sugar, walnuts, and cinnamon; set aside.

When the dough has doubled in bulk, turn onto a floured board and knead until elastic. Pinch off small bits of the dough approximately 1 inch across and shape into balls. Roll balls first in melted butter, then in sugar, walnut, and cinnamon mixture.

Lightly grease the bottom of a tubed pan. Arrange a layer of balls in the buttered tube form several inches apart. Sprinkle 1/3 of the raisins over the top. Arrange a second layer and a third layer in the same way. The tube should be over half full.

Cover with a towel and let rise in a warm place for 20 to 30 minutes. Bake in a preheated oven at 375° for 15 to 20 minutes; turn heat down to 300° and bake until golden.

Loosen the sides with a spatula and turn out on a platter. When serving use two forks to pull apart. Serve hot with any kind of warmed jelly.

Serves 6 to 8

Breads, Rolls and Coffee Cakes

WALNUT CINNAMON ROLL
(Dios Fahellyas Csiga Omlos Tesztabol)

2-3/4 cups all-purpose flour
1-1/4 cups butter
1 tablespoon sugar
1/2 cup milk, lukewarm
1 square yeast
2 egg yolks
2 to 3 tablespoons sour cream

Filling
2 egg whites, beaten stiff
1 cup sugar
2 cups grated nuts
1 teaspoon cinnamon, or 1 tablespoon
   cocoa and 1 teaspoon vanilla

Put flour in a large bowl and cut in butter with a fork or pastry blender until well blended. Combine sugar and milk and dissolve yeast in it. Add to the flour mixture, along with the egg yolks and sour cream. Make a light pastry dough by kneading with your hands until smooth and elastic.

Turn out on a floured board and divide into 2 sections. Cover and let stand in a warm place for 30 minutes.

Meanwhile make filling by folding sugar into well-beaten egg whites; add grated nuts. Add cinnamon or cocoa and vanilla.

Roll out each section the thickness of a match stick. Cover rolled-out dough with filling and roll up. Cut into 1- to 1-1/2-inch slices and put on a baking sheet several inches apart. Bake in an oven preheated at 350° for 20 to 25 minutes or until golden.

This recipe was preserved in my shattered cookbook, along with the childish handwriting of my daughter. It was, and still is, the number one favorite. As Agi wrote, "We cut it in big pieces, we bake it and eat it, but for sure! good and much."

Serves 6 to 8

POPPY-SEED AND NUT ROLLS
(Makos, Diospatko Beigli)

4 cups all-purpose flour
1 pound butter
1/2 cup milk, lukewarm
1 tablespoon sugar
1 cube yeast, or 1 package dry yeast
3 egg yolks
2 to 4 tablespoons sour cream
1 egg, well beaten

Put flour in a large bowl and cut in butter with a fork or pastry blender. Make a well in the center and add milk, sugar, and yeast; mix well until yeast dissolves. Let stand for 5 to 10 minutes or until dough bubbles and rises. Add egg yolks and 2 tablespoons of the sour cream to make a light dough. If needed, add more sour cream.

Turn dough onto a lightly floured board and knead until smooth. Cover with a towel and let stand for 30 minutes. Cut into 4 sections and roll out, one by one. Cover rolled-out pastry with filling, roll up and place in a baking dish. Brush with beaten egg and prick in a few places with a fork or pin. Allow to stand for 20 minutes then brush again with egg. Bake in a preheated oven at 350° for 30 to 45 minutes.

In Hungary every house had poppy-seed and nut rolls to serve guests during the Christmas holidays. Friends often competed to see who made the best ones. They can be kept in a plastic bag in the refrigerator or frozen for several months.

Serves 6 to 8

Walnut Filling
1 cup sugar
3 to 4 tablespoons white wine
1/2 pound ground walnuts
1 tablespoon grated lemon peel
2 to 3 tablespoons apricot or orange jam
1/2 tablespoon cinnamon
1/4 cup raisins
2 tablespoons bread crumbs

Combine sugar and wine and bring to a boil; pour over all other ingredients and mix well.

Poppy-Seed Filling
1 16-ounce can poppy-seed pastry filling
  (Solo Brand)
1 teaspoon grated lemon peel
1 teaspoon vanilla
2 tablespoons jam
1 tablespoon bread crumbs
1/4 cup raisins

Combine all ingredients and mix well. In Hungary we used our own home-grown poppy seeds and ground them with a special grinder. I have found that Solo canned filling is the best substitute. It is available in gourmet food stores or in the gourmet section of your supermarket.

Cookies, Cakes, Desserts and Candies

Along with wine, romance, and gypsy music, the love of pastry and sweets is an important part of traditional Hungarian history. No continental dinner is really complete without a good dessert.

The pastry-making craftsman already belonged to a guild in the Middle Ages and the oldest pastry shop opened in the middle of the 18th century. Probably no other city has so many charming, cozy, pastry shops as Buda and Pest.

Not only people with a sweet tooth, but everybody enjoys talking in the romantic atmosphere of a pastry shop, where each part of the day offers different snacks.

When I translate my pastry recipes, I find the old directions: "Stir vigorously for 1 hour; beat strong a half-hour to get a smooth fluffy texture—the key to a delicious dessert." How much easier it is now with the different speeds of the blessed electric mixers.

As you will see, baking powder is almost never used in Hungarian desserts; instead, lemon juice is substituted which makes a lighter consistency and is healthier.

Try these recipes. You will find their flavors unique and imaginative.

Cookies, Cakes, Desserts and Candies

STRUDEL
(Retes)

In Europe strudel is called the king of pastries. Making the dough is an art and stretching the tissue-thin dough is a fascinating procedure. The most important part of the dough is the rich, glutenous flour produced in Hungary and carefully milled just for this purpose. As it is a tremendous task to make your own dough, I use ready-made phyllo dough. If this dough is handled carefully as advised, you will get as many compliments as I do.

Because the dough is paper thin, you must handle it carefully and quickly before it gets brittle. Have your fillings and 1/2 cup melted butter, and a pastry brush on hand. The butter is brushed between the layers of dough.

There are usually 16 sheets in one package of phyllo dough. Take out only a few sheets at a time and keep the remaining sheets well covered. To use up all the sheets, prepare several fillings. Strudel can be frozen and reheated before serving.

Put a kitchen towel on your cutting board. On this towel is started the foundation of every kind of strudel. Put the first sheet of phyllo dough on the towel and brush it with melted butter; place the second sheet on top and brush it. Repeat this procedure until you have used 4 to 5 sheets of dough. (If the strudel is an appetizer rather than a dessert, use only 2 sheets of dough.) Spread filling on the top of the dough, leaving 3 inches at one side. Roll the strudel up loosely, covering filling, by gently lifting up the towel until it looks like a long sausage.

Place on a buttered baking sheet and flatten slightly with the palm of your hand. Brush top with well-beaten egg. Cut slits in the top about 2-1/2 inches apart. (Don't cut all the way through to the bottom!) Bake in a preheated oven at 375° for 25 to 30 minutes or until strudel is golden. Cut through slits, making individual pieces. Serve fresh and warm.

If the strudel is for dessert, garnish with powdered sugar; if it is an appetizer, garnish with grated cheese.

APPETIZER FILLINGS FOR STRUDEL

When making appetizer strudel, use only 2 sheets of the phyllo dough. Cut slits on the top every 1/2 inch to make bite-sized pieces and use less filling.

Cabbage filling: Shred 1 small cabbage and fry in 4 tablespoons melted butter until limp; season with salt and pepper.

Ham filling: Add 1/2 pound finely chopped ham to thick béchamel sauce (see page 53). Stir in 3 egg yolks and season with salt and pepper. Cool and fold in 3 stiffly beaten egg whites.

Mushroom filling: Wash and slice 1/2 pound mushrooms; sauté in 2 tablespoons butter, along with 2 green onions, finely chopped, and 1 tablespoon parsley. Add to thick béchamel sauce (see page 53). Stir in 3 egg yolks and season with salt and pepper. Cool and fold in 3 stiffly beaten egg whites.

Cheese filling: Add 1 cup grated cheddar cheese to thick béchamel sauce (see page 53). Stir in 3 egg yolks and season with salt and pepper. Cool and fold in 3 stiffly beaten egg whites.

DESSERT FILLINGS FOR STRUDEL

Apple filling: Peel and core 1-1/2 to 2 pounds apples; slice thin. Combine apples, 1/2 cup raisins, and 1 tablespoon grated lemon rind. Combine 1 teaspoon cinnamon, 1 cup sugar, and 1 cup grated walnuts or 3/4 cup bread crumbs. Top dough with the nut and sugar mixture and then with the apple mixture.

Cherry filling: Drain a 16-ounce can of pitted, sour cherries well. Combine with 1/2 cup raisins. Combine 1 cup sugar and 1 cup grated walnuts. Top dough first with the nut and sugar mixture and then with the cherry mixture. (The amount of sugar depends on the tartness of the fruit and your own individual taste.)

Baker's cheese filling: Beat 3 egg whites until stiff; add 1/4 cup sugar and beat 2 to 3 minutes. Cream together 3 egg yolks, 1/2 to 3/4 cup sugar to taste, and 1 teaspoon vanilla until thick and fluffy. Add 1 pound baker's cheese and 2 tablespoons cream of wheat; stir until well blended. Carefully fold in 3 egg whites, 1/2 cup white raisins, and 1 teaspoon grated lemon peel.

Cookies, Cakes, Desserts and Candies

ISCHL COOKIES I
(Ischler)

1-1/2 cups sifted, all-purpose flour
1/2 cup ground hazelnuts
3/4 cup unsalted butter
1 teaspoon vanilla
1/2 teaspoon lemon juice
3/4 cup sugar
raspberry jam
15 to 20 blanched almonds
chocolate frosting (see page 171)

Combine flour, hazelnuts, and butter in a bowl; blend well with a fork or pastry blender. Add vanilla, lemon juice, and sugar; knead into a smooth dough. Cover and chill in refrigerator.

Roll dough onto a lightly floured board about 1/4 inch thick. Cut into rounds with a cookie cutter and bake in a preheated oven at 350° for 15 to 20 minutes or until golden.

Cool and make sandwiches, filling with jam. Place cookies on a cooling rack and pour a spoonful of chocolate frosting over each. (It is good to put foil under the rack so that the drippings can be returned to the frosting pan.) Place a blanched almond in the middle of each cookie.

There are quite a number of variations around these cookies which were highly favored by our former Emperor and King of Austria-Hungary, Franz Josef. They named the cookies after a summer resort in the Austrian Alps where the King spent his leisure time.

LINZER WREATH COOKIES
(Linzer Koszoruk)

3/4 cup sugar
2-2/3 cups all-purpose flour
1/2 pound butter
3 egg yolks
1 to 2 tablespoons rum
3 to 4 tablespoons sour cream
1 teaspoon vanilla
1/4 cup finely chopped walnuts
1/4 cup powdered sugar
1 egg, slightly beaten
raspberry jam

Put sugar and flour in a bowl; cut in butter with a fork or pastry blender. When well blended add egg yolks, rum, sour cream, and vanilla. Knead with hands until smooth. Shape into a ball with the palms of your hands and chill in the refrigerator (it is preferable to chill overnight).

Combine nuts and powdered sugar; set aside. Roll the dough 1/8 to 1/4 inch thick on a lightly floured board. Cut dough into rounds or any other desired shape with a floured cookie cutter. Brush cookies with the beaten egg and dip into the nut-sugar mixture. Bake in a preheated oven at 350° for 15 to 20 minutes or until lightly browned. Sprinkle cookies with powdered sugar. Turn half of the cookies upside down and spread with jam. Make cookie sandwiches by placing remaining cookies on top.

Variation: Linzer Crescents (Linzer Kifli) Roll a third of the dough 1/4 inch thick. Cut into big rounds with a cookie cutter and spread desired filling of jam, or nuts, or poppy seeds, or chestnuts on top. Fold dough over mixture into the shape of a crescent. Brush with a slightly beaten egg and bake in a preheated oven at 375° for 20 to 25 minutes or until lightly golden. Sprinkle with vanilla-flavored powdered sugar.

Variation: Ischl Cookies II Add 1/4 teaspoon cinnamon, 1 teaspoon cocoa, and 3 teaspoons ground hazelnuts to a third of the dough; work in with the palms of your hands. Roll dough 1/4 inch thick. Cut into rounds with a cookie cutter and bake at 350° for 15 to 20 minutes or until lightly browned. When cool turn half of the cookies upside down and spread about 1/2 teaspoon tart jam on each. Make cookie sandwiches by placing remaining cookies on top. Set aside.

Melt semi-sweet chocolate with 1 to 2 teaspoons fine oil in a double boiler. Dip tops of cookies into chocolate. Place cookies on a cooling rack and put half a blanched almond on each.

Variation: Latticed Linzer Pastry (Racsos Linzer) Roll a third of the dough 1/4 inch thick in the shape of a baking pan. Spread dough in the pan so that the bottom is covered. Spread ground nuts mixed with sugar and ground cinnamon over the top. Spoon jam (any kind that is tart) over to completely cover. Roll the remaining dough thin and cut in strips; crisscross over jam. Bake in a preheated oven at 350° for 25 to 30 minutes. When cool, cut into square or rectangular shapes.

VANILLA CRESCENT
(Vanilias Kifli)

1/2 pound butter
2/3 cup sugar
1/2 teaspoon salt
1-3/4 cups all-purpose flour
5 ounces grated almonds
vanilla-flavored powdered sugar

Put butter, sugar, and salt in a bowl and cream well. Add flour and almonds and knead until smooth. Turn dough onto a lightly floured board and shape into small crescents. Place on a buttered, floured baking sheet.

Bake in a preheated oven at 375° for 15 to 20 minutes or until lightly golden. Carefully remove from baking sheet; the cookies are very fragile. Roll in powdered sugar while still warm.

If your chocolate frosting bowl is not empty, dunk the ends in chocolate. This adds to the flavor and appearance.

Cookies, Cakes, Desserts and Candies

ZWIEBACK
(Ketszersult)

6 large eggs, separated
1 cup sugar
1/2 teaspoon cream of tartar
1 teaspoon vanilla
2 tablespoons warm water
1 cup all-purpose flour
1/2 cup blanched almonds, halved
vanilla-flavored powdered sugar

Beat egg whites until stiff; add 1/4 cup sugar and cream of tartar. Cream egg yolks with remaining sugar, vanilla and water. Carefully fold in flour, almonds, and egg whites.

Put dough in a meat-loaf pan and bake in a preheated oven at 350° for 20 to 30 minutes. Cover and cool on a rack.

Leave zwieback at room temperature for 3 days and then cut into 1/2-inch slices. Put slices on a baking sheet and toast in a preheated oven at 350° for 10 to 15 minutes or until golden. Turn slices during baking so they will be evenly browned. Remove from oven and dust generously with vanilla-flavored powdered sugar. Keep well covered in a cool place.

It's very good to have zwieback on hand at any time, as they are excellent with tea, coffee, or ice cream.

Serves 6 to 8

WOOD SHAVING COOKIES
(Forgacs Fank)

2 cups flour
1/2 teaspoon salt
1 tablespoon sugar
3 egg yolks, slightly beaten
1/2 cup sour cream
1/2 teaspoon vanilla
1 tablespoon rum
vegetable oil for deep frying
vanilla-flavored powdered sugar
jelly

Sift flour, salt, and sugar together into a bowl. Make a well in the center. Combine egg yolks, sour cream, vanilla, and rum and pour into the dry ingredients. Blend until all the flour is moistened. Let dough stand for 30 minutes.

Turn dough onto a lightly floured board and knead until smooth. Divide dough into 2 parts and roll 1/8 inch thick with a floured rolling pin. Cut rolled dough into 1-inch strips with a pastry cutter and deep fry in fine oil, turning when golden brown. Be careful that the oil does not get too hot. Do not fry too many cookies at one time so they will brown evenly. Remove with a fork or tongs, draining over the pan, and put on paper towels.

Sprinkle cookies with vanilla-flavored powdered sugar and serve with warmed jelly. This dough can be prepared days ahead and kept in a plastic bag in the refrigerator. Roll and deep fry when ready to use.

Cookies, Cakes, Desserts and Candies

VIENNESE SQUARES
(Becsi Szelet)

2-1/4 cups all-purpose flour
2/3 cup sugar
1/2 pound butter
1 teaspoon cinnamon
1 egg
1 3-1/2-ounce package hazelnuts, ground
powdered sugar for dusting

Filling
1/4 pound butter
2/3 cup sugar
1 egg
2 tablespoons rum
1 3-1/2-ounce package walnuts, ground

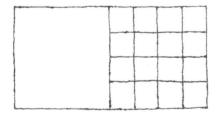

Put flour and sugar in a bowl; cut in butter with a fork or pastry blender. Add cinnamon, egg, and hazelnuts; knead together lightly with your hands. Form into a loaf, cover with waxed paper, and chill in the refrigerator for 1 hour.

Place dough in a 9x16-inch baking pan and flatten with your hand until about 1/2 inch high and covering the bottom of the pan. Bake in a preheated oven several minutes at 350°, watching carefully. When sides begin to turn golden, remove from oven, leave in pan, and immediately cut half of the dough into 2-inch squares with a sharp, thin-bladed knife.

Prepare filling by creaming all ingredients together. When fluffy spread on the uncut half of the cooled pastry. Put cut squares over the filling to completely cover. (Making the squares in this way makes it easier to cut the squares through without squeezing out the filling.)

This is one of the greatest heritages from our neighboring Vienna.

HUNGARIAN LOVE LETTERS
(Szerelmes Level)

2-2/3 cups all-purpose flour
1-1/4 cups butter
1 whole egg plus 1 egg yolk
1/2 cup cold milk
1 3-1/2-ounce package walnuts, grated
3/4 cup sugar
1/2 cup graham-cracker crumbs
1 teaspoon cinnamon
1/2 cup raisins, washed and dried
2-1/2 pounds green apples, washed,
  peeled, cored, and shredded
1 egg, slightly beaten

Put flour in a large bowl; cut in butter with a fork or pastry blender until the mixture makes small balls. Add eggs and milk and mix well. Gather dough into a ball and turn onto a lightly floured board. Knead dough with hands until smooth; form into the shape of a sausage and roll in waxed paper. Refrigerate 1 to 2 hours or, preferably, overnight.

Divide dough into 3 parts. Roll out each section to fit an 11x18-inch baking dish. Line dough to fit and cover both the bottom and the sides of the pan. Mix grated nuts with sugar, crumbs, and cinnamon. Use two-thirds of this mixture to spread on and cover the first layer of dough. Put raisins evenly over the top and cover with the second layer of dough. Mix shredded apples with remaining nut mixture and put over the second layer of dough. Cover apple filling with the third layer of dough and brush twice over with the beaten egg.

Make lines in the dough with a fork dipped in warm water. Bake in a preheated oven at 350° for 30 to 35 minutes or until evenly browned. Let cool on a rack for several hours and cut into squares or oblongs in an envelope shape.

I made a great success with this very excellent pastry when I baked several hundred batches for one of the best gourmet delicatessens in San Francisco during the course of a year. This was a great experience and added a new chapter to my life.

Serves 8

Cookies, Cakes, Desserts and Candies

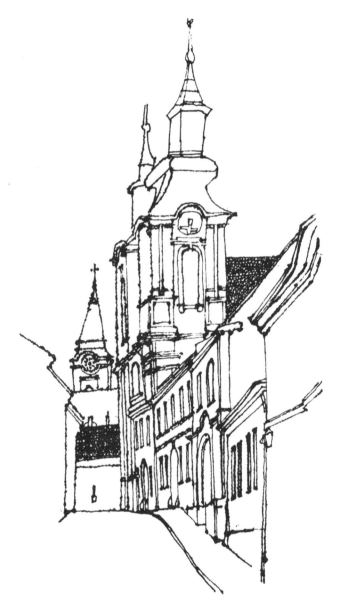

TURKISH SLICE
(Torok Lepeny)

3/4 cup butter
1 cup plus 2 tablespoons sugar
7 eggs, separated
2 cups all-purpose flour
1/4 cup grated almonds
2 squares Baker's semi-sweet chocolate, melted
apricot jam

Cream together butter, 2 tablespoons sugar, and 3 egg yolks; add flour and knead into a smooth dough. Spread dough evenly in a 9x16-inch baking pan with your hand. (Put flour on your palm to make it easier to smooth the sticky dough.)

Bake in a 350° oven for several minutes until edges start to turn golden. Remove from oven.

Beat 7 egg whites until stiff; fold in almonds and set aside in a cool place. Cream together 4 egg yolks and 1 cup sugar; when fluffy add chocolate and fold in egg-white mixture.

Spread surface of dough with apricot jam; cover evenly with the chocolate-nut-egg mixture. Return to oven for 20 to 25 minutes.

Cool and slice as much as needed. If well covered, this pastry will stay fresh a long time.

Turkish slices are another reminder of the time the Turks ruled Hungary.

Serves 8

SHAUMTORTE, PASTRY SHELLS OR KISSES
(Habcsok)

3 egg whites
1 cup sugar
1 tablespoon water
1 teaspoon vanilla
1 teaspoon vinegar
halved walnuts (optional)
chocolate chips (optional)

Beat egg whites until stiff; gradually add sugar. Beat again adding water, vanilla, and vinegar. Shape into small forms, adding some chopped walnuts or chocolate chips to the mixture, if desired.

Preheat oven to 250°; reduce heat and bake at 200° for 1 hour. When using this recipe, use egg whites saved from wood shaving cookies (page 144).

Variation: Make pastry shells from the same mixture with a decorating bag and bake the same way. Fill with fruit, ice cream, custard, or chestnut rice (see page 175).

ALMOND KISSES
(Mandulas Puszedli)

3 egg whites
1 3-1/2-ounce package walnuts, ground
1 cup sugar
3 tablespoons all-purpose flour
1 teaspoon vanilla
1 teaspoon grated lemon rind
1/2 teaspoon almond extract
1 3-1/2-ounce package slivered almonds

Put egg whites, nuts, and sugar in a double boiler; stir until hot and ingredients melt together. Remove from heat and mix in flour, vanilla, lemon rind, and almond extract. Set aside until mixture cools and thickens. Wet your hands and shape dough into little balls; roll in slivered almonds. Put several inches apart on a baking sheet lined with waxed paper. Let stand for several hours.

Preheat oven to 250°; reduce heat to 200° and bake for 30 minutes or until easily removed from waxed paper.

Serves 6

Cookies, Cakes, Desserts and Candies

CRACKLING BISCUITS
(Toportyus Pogacsa)

2-1/2 cups all-purpose flour
1/4 pound butter
1/2 cup sour cream
1 egg yolk
1 square yeast, crumbled
1 pound bacon
salt and pepper to taste
1 egg, slightly beaten

Put flour in a bowl; cut in 4 tablespoons butter with a fork or pastry blender. Make a well in the center and add sour cream, egg yolk, and yeast; mix well until yeast dissolves. Turn onto a floured board and knead until shiny and elastic. Cover with a dish towel and let stand for 30 minutes.

Fry bacon crisp, drain, and crumble into a bowl; add 4 tablespoons melted butter, salt, and pepper, and mix well.

Roll dough out and spread half the bacon mixture on top. Fold the dough in half, covering mixture, and let stand 30 minutes. Roll out again and spread second half of the bacon mixture on top. Let stand for 30 minutes and roll out 1 inch thick. Cut with a round biscuit cutter and place biscuits on a cookie sheet several inches apart. Score a crisscross pattern on top with a sharp knife and brush with the beaten egg. Let stand for 30 minutes to an hour. Brush with egg again and bake in a preheated oven for 5 minutes at 475°; lower temperature to 375° and continue baking for 10 to 15 minutes or until golden brown.

Serve these highly seasoned, warm biscuits with wine, as they increase your thirst.

Serves 6 to 8

Cookies, Cakes, Desserts and Candies

SALTY TEA BISCUITS
(Sos Tea Sutemeny)

3 cups all-purpose flour
1 teaspoon salt
3/4 pound butter
1-1/2 squares yeast, crumbled
3 egg yolks
1/2 cup sour cream
1 egg, slightly beaten

Put flour and salt in a bowl; cut in butter with a fork or pastry blender. Make a well in the center and add yeast, egg yolks, and sour cream; mix well until yeast dissolves.

Knead into a smooth shiny dough and turn onto a lightly floured board. Roll out 1/2 to 3/4 inch thick. Place dough on waxed paper, brush top with beaten egg, and make long lines across the top with a fork dipped into hot water; brush again with egg and chill 24 hours in the refrigerator.

Remove dough from refrigerator and brush with egg. Cut into different shapes with a sharp knife. (Cut only as many biscuits as you will need. The unbaked dough can be stored in the refrigerator for 2 to 3 days. Fresh-baked are the best.)

Decorate biscuits with any of the following: poppy seeds, salt and caraway seeds, grated cheese and paprika, or halved almonds. Preheat oven to 400° and bake at 375° for 20 to 25 minutes or until biscuits are golden.

This is originally the recipe of our most famous pastry chef, Gerbeaud. In his shop in Budapest you could find the biggest variety of pastries for gourmet tastes. These are the small biscuits that are served with the forenoon vermouth, as well as with the afternoon tea.

Serves 6 to 8

BASIC SPONGE CAKE
(Piskota)

sweet butter
6 eggs, separated
1 cup sugar
1 tablespoon lemon juice
1 cup all-purpose flour

Cover a 9x16-inch pan with foil and brush with soft butter. Beat egg whites until stiff; beat in 1/3 of the sugar until rounded peaks are formed. Using the same beater, beat egg yolks, lemon, and remaining sugar until lemon colored; carefully fold into egg whites, alternately with flour. Do not overmix!

Pour into the baking pan and bake in a preheated oven at 325° for 35 minutes, or until a light touch leaves no impression.

Variation: Jelly Roll If the sponge cake is to be used for a jelly roll, turn the baked cake (including the foil) onto a floured dish towel. Roll up. Cool, unroll, and peel off foil. Fill jelly roll with any kind of jelly or whipped cream. Sprinkle powdered sugar on top or spread thinly with jam or chocolate frosting and sprinkle with slivered almonds.

If the sponge cake is unfrosted, it is very good served with wine sauce (following). In our family the unfilled jelly roll is called a "bracelet cake." In order to introduce the grandchildren to a new type of food, I put one of the unfilled jelly rolls on their wrists like a bracelet and it became their favorite.

Variation: Strawberry Shortcake Divide sponge cake batter evenly and bake in two pie pans at 325° for 25 to 30 minutes. Cool and sprinkle with rum; top with whipped cream and strawberries. Place on top of each other to make a layer cake.

Serves 6 to 8

WINE SAUCE
(Bor Martas)

3 eggs
1/2 cup sugar
juice of 1 lemon
1 cup white wine

Combine eggs and sugar and beat until thick and lemon colored. Put in a double boiler, add wine and lemon juice, and continue beating over boiling water until thickened. Serve hot or chilled. If served chilled, put individual servings into wine glasses while sauce is still warm.

This sauce improves every simple or dry sponge-cake pastry.

Cookies, Cakes, Desserts and Candies

HUNGARIAN CHEESE CAKE
(Turo Torta)

1-1/2 cups all-purpose flour
3/4 cup butter
1 tablespoon lemon juice
4 eggs, separated, plus 2 egg yolks
1-1/2 tablespoons sour cream
2 medium-sized potatoes
1-1/4 cups sugar
1 pound baker's cheese
1-1/2 teaspoons vanilla
2 tablespoons milk
1 tablespoon cream of wheat
1/2 cup white raisins
1 teaspoon grated lemon rind
10 to 12 blanched almonds, sliced

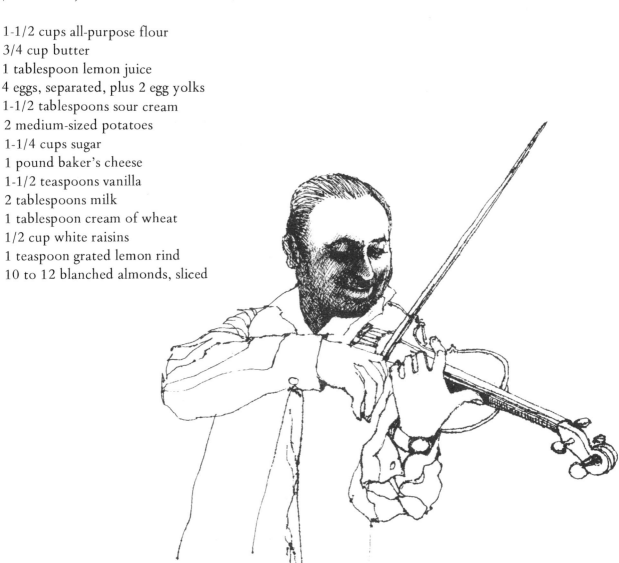

Put flour in a bowl; cut in 1/4 pound butter with a fork or pastry blender. Add the lemon juice 2 egg yolks, and sour cream; knead until you have a smooth dough. Form dough into a ball, cover with waxed paper, and put in the refrigerator.

Cook the potatoes in their skins, peel, and put through a potato ricer. Let cool.

Combine 4 egg yolks, sugar, and 4 table-spoons butter; stir until creamy. Add baker's cheese and stir again; add vanilla, milk, cold potatoes, and cream of wheat. Beat 4 egg whites until stiff and fold in, with the raisins and lemon rind.

Remove dough from the refrigerator and roll into a circle 1/4 inch thick. (Save 1/3 of the dough for making strips.) Cover bottom and sides of a 8- to 9-inch spring cake pan with dough. Pour cheese mixture into lined cake pan and put strips of dough crosswise on the top. Garnish with sliced almonds and bake in a preheated oven at 350° for 30 minutes; lower heat to 300° and bake another 30 minutes.

Serve lukewarm. This dessert is ever so good after a fish meal or with coffee. It is less rich than the cream cheese version and twice as good.

ALMOND CAKE
(Mandula Torta)

7 egg whites
1 cup sugar
1/2 pound blanched almonds

Filling
7 egg yolks
3/4 cup sugar
1 teaspoon vanilla
2 squares Baker's semi-sweet chocolate, melted
3/4 cup sweet butter, creamed
1 tablespoon cointreau liqueur
1 square chocolate for garnish

Beat egg whites until stiff; add sugar, beating constantly. Fold in almonds. Bake in a 9x9-inch spring cake form or a 9x16-inch baking pan in a preheated oven at 350° for 25 to 30 minutes. Cool cake on a rack.

Combine egg yolks, sugar, and vanilla in a double boiler and stir until thick; add chocolate. Cool and add creamed butter and liqueur.

If baked in the 9x9-inch cake form, cut into layers and spread cream filling between layers and on top of the cake. If baked in a 9x16-inch baking pan, cut lengthwise into 3 strips; spread cream filling on each strip and on the top. Garnish with chocolate shavings, scraping chocolate evenly over cake with a knife.

DIVINE CHOCOLATE ROULADE
(Remek Gesztenyes Tekercs)

6 eggs, separated
6 heaping tablespoons sugar
6 tablespoons flour, or 3 tablespoons flour plus
   3 tablespoons ground nuts
1 heaping tablespoon cocoa

Filling
3 eggs
3 heaping tablespoons sugar
1/2 envelope unflavored gelatin
2 tablespoons cold water
1 8-ounce can crème de marrons (chestnuts)
1/2 pint whipping cream
2 tablespoons rum
chocolate shavings or slivered almonds for garnish

Beat egg whites until stiff; add 2 tablespoons sugar and beat again until firm. Mix egg yolks and 4 tablespoons sugar until lemon colored. Gently fold in flour, nuts (if used) and cocoa, alternately with egg whites. Put dough in a 11-1/2x15-1/2-inch baking pan lined with well-buttered foil. Bake in a preheated oven at 325° for 20 to 25 minutes. Test for doneness with a needle or toothpick. Remove from oven and roll up (including foil) in a floured kitchen towel. Set aside.

To make filling mix eggs and sugar in a double boiler until thick. Add gelatin which has been dissolved in cold water. Remove from heat and add chestnut purée. When completely cool add whipped cream.

Unfold cake, removing foil, and put filling in the center (holding out a little for topping). Reroll and put on a long tray; sprinkle with rum. Decorate top with leftover filling. Make star shapes using a decorator sack or spread on top and garnish with chocolate shavings or slivered almonds.

Serves 6 to 8

MOCHA CAKE
(Mokka Torta)

6 eggs, separated
2/3 cup sugar
1 tablespoon lemon juice
3 tablespoons all-purpose flour

Filling
1 square Baker's semi-sweet chocolate
1 tablespoon instant coffee
1/2 cup coffee
3/4 cup sweet butter
1 egg
2/3 cup sugar
1 tablespoon vanilla
1 3-1/2-ounce package blanched almonds for
  garnish, cut in tiny squares

Beat egg whites until stiff; add 2 to 3 tablespoons sugar. Cream together egg yolks, remaining sugar, and lemon juice until lemon colored and fluffy; fold in egg whites alternately with flour.

Bake in a 9x16-inch baking pan in a preheated oven at 350° for 10 minutes; lower heat to 300° and bake for 20 minutes or until golden. Cool on a cake rack and cut lengthwise into 3 pieces.

In a saucepan combine chocolate, instant coffee, and 1/2 cup coffee and heat until chocolate melts; let simmer for 5 minutes and cool. Cream together butter, egg, sugar, and vanilla; gradually add cooled coffee mixture and beat well. Spread filling between layers and over top and sides.

Toast almonds in 1 to 2 tablespoons sugar on low heat; when brown remove from flame and stir with a fork until cool so they won't stick together. Decorate top of the cake with the almonds—they are not only pretty but add to the flavor as well.

Serves 6 to 8

DATE CAKE
(Datolya Torta)

5 egg whites
3/4 cup sugar
1 3-1/2-ounce package blanched almonds, ground
2 tablespoons mixed candied fruit
1 tablespoon fine bread crumbs
1/4 pound sliced, pitted dates

Filling
5 egg yolks
2/3 cup sugar
2 squares Baker's semi-sweet chocolate
2 tablespoons instant coffee
1/2 cup strong coffee
1 envelope gelatin
1/2 cup warm water
1-1/2 cups whipping cream, whipped
1 3-1/2-ounce package slivered almonds

Beat egg whites until stiff; add sugar and beat well. Fold in almonds, fruit, bread crumbs, and dates. Bake in a well-buttered and floured 9x9-inch spring-form cake pan in a preheated oven at 350° for 25 to 30 minutes. Cool on a rack in the pan.

Combine egg yolks, sugar, chocolate, instant coffee, and coffee in a double boiler; stir constantly until thick. Melt gelatin in warm water and add to the double boiler. Remove from heat and cool; fold in whipped cream and pour over cooled cake, leaving cake in the pan.

Put in the refrigerator overnight. Loosen edges of cake from pan with a knife and put onto a serving platter. Garnish sides with slivered almonds.

Variation: a simpler version Bake cake in a 9x11-inch baking pan. Cut lengthwise into 2 layers; fill and top with whipped cream. Sprinkle cake with 2 tablespoons rum and garnish with slivered almonds.

Serves 6 to 8

Cookies, Cakes, Desserts and Candies

BLITZ TORTE
(Villam Torta)

1 cup all-purpose flour
1 teaspoon baking powder
1/4 pound butter
1/2 cup sugar
5 eggs, separated
1 teaspoon vanilla
3 tablespoons milk
1 cup powdered sugar
1 cup slivered almonds

Sift flour and baking powder together. Cream butter with sugar until fluffy; add egg yolks, vanilla, milk, and sifted flour. Spread into two 9x9-inch baking pans and set aside.

Beat egg whites until stiff; gradually add sugar, beating well. Spread over unbaked dough in both cake pans and sprinkle with almonds. Bake in a preheated oven at 350° for 10 minutes; lower heat to 300° and bake 20 minutes. Cool on a cake rack and spread filling between layers. I usually use a tart red currant jam or a vanilla custard.

Custard: Combine 2 egg yolks, 1/2 cup sugar, 1/2 cup milk, 2 tablespoons flour, and 1 teaspoon vanilla in a double boiler and stir until thick. Cool and add 2 well-beaten egg whites and more vanilla, if desired.

Serves 6

PARFAIT TORTE
(Parfe Torta)

2 3-ounce packages lady fingers
1-1/2 cups milk
1/2 cup rum
2/3 cup sugar
4 egg yolks
2 tablespoons all-purpose flour
1 teaspoon vanilla
1/4 pound butter
1 3-1/2-ounce package almonds or walnuts, grated
1/2 pint whipping cream for topping
candied fruit for garnish

Line a 9-inch spring-form cake pan with half of the lady fingers, along sides and bottom. Mix 1/2 cup milk with 1/4 cup rum and sprinkle over lady fingers. Combine remaining milk, 1/3 cup sugar, egg yolks, flour, and vanilla in a double boiler and stir until thick. Cool.

Cream together butter and 1/3 cup sugar. Add cooled flour mixture and ground nuts; beat until fluffy. Gradually add the remaining rum. Carefully pour cream mixture over lady fingers so that they remain well-arranged. Cover with second half of lady fingers and refrigerate overnight.

When ready to serve, turn onto a serving plate and top with whipped cream and candied fruit.

Serves 8

SACHER TORTE
(Sacher Torta)

5 eggs, separated
1/2 cup sugar
4 squares Baker's semi-sweet chocolate, grated
2 tablespoons fine bread crumbs
1 3-1/2-ounce package almonds,
    filberts, or other nuts, ground
1/4 pound butter, melted and cooled
red currant or raspberry jam
chocolate frosting (see page 171)
whipping cream

Beat egg whites until stiff; add 1/3 of the sugar and continue beating until rounded peaks are formed. With the same beater, beat egg yolks with remaining sugar until fluffy and lemon colored. Fold grated chocolate, bread crumbs, egg whites, and nuts into the egg yolk mixture until mixed well. Then gently fold in butter.

Bake in a 8x8-inch cake pan in a preheated oven at 350° for 15 minutes; lower heat to 300° and continue baking for 30 minutes or until done. Cake is done when a light touch leaves no impression; or test with a needle or toothpick.

Put cake on a rack to cool. Run spatula gently around the sides and turn cake onto a platter. When completely cool, spread jam over the top and sides and pour chocolate icing over. Serve with whipped cream.

This is believed to be the original and best recipe from the famous Sacher Hotel in Vienna. This hotel was once the meeting place of the high class and elegant with a gourmet taste.

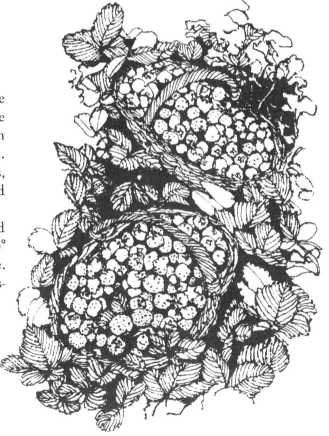

CHESTNUT TORTE
(Gesztenye Torta)

2 pounds chestnuts
milk as needed
6 eggs, separated
1 cup sugar
1 tablespoon fine bread crumbs
chocolate frosting (see page 171)
1/2 pint whipping cream for topping

Filling
1/4 pound butter
1 egg
2 tablespoons rum
2 tablespoons sugar

Put chestnuts in a large saucepan and cover with water; boil for 10 minutes. Remove outer and inner peel from chestnuts; take only a few out of the water at a time, as they are easier to peel when warm. Cover peeled chestnuts with milk and simmer until tender and milk is absorbed; press chestnuts through a sieve.

Beat egg whites until stiff; add 1/3 of the sugar and beat 2 to 3 more minutes. Set aside.

Cream together egg yolks and remaining sugar until lemon colored. Fold in egg whites alternately with half of the chestnuts (which replace flour) and the bread crumbs.

Put in a well-buttered and floured 8x9-inch baking pan. Bake in a preheated oven at 350° for 30 to 35 minutes or until a light touch leaves no impression.

When cake is completely cool split into 2 layers. Combine filling ingredients with remaining chestnuts and spread over bottom layer; cover with top layer. Pour chocolate frosting over the top and decorate the sides with whipped cream squeezed from a decorating bag.

Serves 6 to 8

LEMON TORTE
(Citrom Torta)

6 large eggs, separated
1 cup sugar
juice and grated rind of 1 lemon
2/3 cup cake flour

Filling
2-1/4 cups milk
1/4 cup all-purpose flour
3/4 cup butter
3/4 cup vanilla-flavored powdered sugar
currant jelly
1/2 cup blanched almonds, grated
candied lemon peel for garnish

Beat egg whites until stiff; gradually add 1/3 cup sugar, beating well. Set aside in a cool place.

Combine egg yolks, 2/3 cup sugar, and lemon juice; beat until thick and lemon colored. Fold in egg whites alternately with flour and lemon rind.

Bake in a well-buttered and floured 9x16-inch baking pan in a preheated oven at 350° for 25 to 30 minutes.

To make filling bring 2 cups milk to a boil; combine remaining milk and flour to make a smooth paste and add to the hot milk, stirring constantly until mixture thickens. Remove from heat and cool. Cream butter and sugar together and add to milk; beat until fluffy.

Cut cake lengthwise into 3 strips. Spread first the currant jelly and then the cream filling on the first strip; place second strip on top and repeat. Cover with third strip and spread currant jelly and cream on top and sides. Sprinkle with almonds and garnish with candied lemon peel.

This has always been the birthday cake for my younger daughter and is still her number-one favorite.

Serves 6 to 8

Cookies, Cakes, Desserts and Candies

PUNCH TORTE
(Puncs Torta)

Cake
8 eggs, separated
1 cup sugar
1 cup all-purpose flour
1 teaspoon vanilla
1 tablespoon lemon juice
1 teaspoon grated lemon rind

Filling
1/2 cup rum
1/2 cup sugar
1/4 cup water
juice of 1/2 lemon
juice of 1 orange
3 teaspoons cocoa
1 cup ground walnuts
1 teaspoon vanilla
2 tablespoons orange marmalade
3 to 4 tablespoons apricot jam
2 tablespoons candied fruit, cut into small pieces

Make cake batter as directed for the sponge cake (see page 153). Bake half of the sponge cake batter in a 8x9-inch cake pan. Bake the second half of the batter in a 9x16-inch cake pan. (Batter should be about 1-1/2 inches high.) Cool cakes; cut 8x9-inch cake into 2 layers and set aside.

Cut 9x16-inch cake into cubes and sprinkle with rum. Combine sugar and water in a small saucepan and stir over low heat until it begins to thicken. Remove from heat and add lemon and orange juice, cocoa, nuts, vanilla, and orange marmalade; pour over cake cubes. Turn with a spatula to evenly moisten cubes; be careful not to crush or break the cubes.

Put the first half of the round cake back into the cake pan and spread with 1/2 of the apricot jam. Put moistened cake cubes on top and flatten slightly with a spatula.

Spread candied fruit on top and cover with the second half of the apricot jam. Top with second half of cake.

Cover cake with waxed paper and place a plate or lid on the top with some weight; refrigerate for one day.

Ice on the day of serving.

Icing for Punch Torte (Punes Torta Maz)
2-1/2 cups powdered sugar
1-1/2 tablespoons water
1 tablespoon lemon juice
1 tablespoon rum
2 to 3 drops red food coloring
blanched almonds or maraschino
   cherries for decoration

Combine sugar and water in a saucepan and cook over low heat until mixture begins to thicken. Remove from heat and add lemon juice, rum, and food coloring; mix well.

Spread on cake while still warm, using a spatula or wide-bladed knife. Have hot water on hand to dip your knife in; this helps the icing spread evenly over the cake. If icing seems too runny, add more powdered sugar.

Decorate top of cake with cherries or almonds.

Serves 8

GYPSY JOHN
(Rigo Jancsi)

6 large eggs, separated
1 cup sugar
1/2 cup all-purpose flour
1/2 cup cocoa
2 to 3 tablespoons currant jelly
chocolate frosting (see page 171)

Filling
1 pint whipping cream
1/2 cup cocoa
1/2 to 3/4 cup sugar
2 tablespoons rum

This cake recipe can be multiplied by 1-1/2 or doubled for a larger cake; vary colander size accordingly.

Beat egg whites until stiff; add 1/4 cup sugar and beat for 2 minutes. Set aside in a cool place.

Cream together egg yolks and remaining sugar; fold in flour and cocoa alternately with the egg whites.

This cake is traditionally baked on a baking sheet, but I use a metal colander to get a very impressive and unusual effect. Line the insides of a 9-inch colander with well-buttered foil paper. Add mixture and bake in a preheated oven at 350° for 15 minutes; turn down heat to 325° and bake for 30 to 35 minutes or until done. If a light touch leaves no impression, the cake is done.

Cool cake, leaving it in the colander. Cut the top of the cake off in the shape of a circle about 1 inch deep; set aside. Carefully scoop out the insides of the cake, leaving a 1-inch crust all around.

Make filling by whipping cream until stiff; gently fold in cocoa and sugar to taste. Sprinkle the scooped-out cake with rum; put 3/4 of the filling into the cake cavity, along with the sliced insides of the cake. Cover with the cut-off top.

(A separate dessert can be made with the leftover cake. Cut into cubes and sprinkle with rum. Top with chocolate sauce or whipped cream.)

Turn cake onto a platter and carefully peel off the foil. Spread outsides with currant jelly (this is like a cosmetic to cover up the wrinkles made by the foil). Pour chocolate frosting over the top and cool in the refrigerator. When frosting is hard, decorate the cake with the remaining filling, using a decorator bag. This is a gorgeous and excellent cake for very special occasions. It is wise to prepare it a day ahead. At the table, slice into melon shapes with a sharp knife.

This cake has a true story that goes with it. The tale dates back to 1895 when Gypsy John seduced a young princess with his brilliant violin playing. She left her prince and ran away with the gypsy. This created a great scandal and the biggest gossip of the time. One smart chef used this romance to create a cake. He made the cake dark like the gypsy and it turned out to be one of the biggest successes of all Hungarian cakes.

Serves from 6 to 10

WALNUT SLICES
(Dios Szelet)

6 egg whites
1-1/2 cups sugar
4 ounces walnuts, ground
2/3 cup butter
2 egg yolks
1/3 cup sugar
1 tablespoon lemon juice
1 teaspoon vanilla
1-1/2 cups all-purpose flour
apricot jam

Beat egg whites until stiff; slowly add 1-1/2 cups sugar, stirring constantly. Fold in ground walnuts and set aside.

Cream together butter, egg yolks, and 1/3 cup sugar; add lemon juice and vanilla and beat until fluffy. Add flour and mix well. Spread dough evenly in a 9x16-inch baking pan with your hand—put flour on your palm to make it easier to smooth the sticky dough.

Bake several minutes in a preheated oven at 350° until dough is set and edges begin to turn golden. Remove from oven and spread a thin layer of apricot jam on top; spread egg-white mixture over with a spatula. Bake for 25 to 30 minutes or until golden. When completely cool, slice with a sharp knife into small oblongs. Slice only what you need. If well covered or put in an airtight container, these will stay fresh for a long time.

Serves 6 to 8

PYRAMID WITH CHOCOLATE SAUCE
(Piramis Csokolade Szosszal)

sponge cake (see page 153), doubled
1/2 cup milk
1/4 cup rum
1/2 cup sugar
1-1/2 pints whipping cream

Topping:
1/2 cup sugar
4 squares Baker's semi-sweet chocolate
1 cup strong coffee

Use sponge cake recipe and bake in 2 9x16-inch baking pans. When cake is cool, cut out a 7x7-inch square, a 6x6-inch square, a 5x5-inch square, a 4x4-inch square, a 3x3-inch square, a 2x2-inch square, and a 1x1-inch square. I have a waxed-paper pattern for each size which I arrange on top of the sponge cake and cut around.

(A separate dessert can be made with the leftover cake. Cut into cubes and sprinkle with rum. Top with chocolate sauce or whipped cream.)

Combine milk and rum and set aside. Fold sugar into whipped cream and set aside.

Put the 7x7-inch square on a cake platter and sprinkle with the milk and rum mixture. Spread whipped cream and sugar mixture on top, about 1-1/2-inches high. Put the 6x6-inch square on top and repeat procedure until you have the shape of a pyramid. Smooth remaining whipped cream on the sides with a wide-bladed knife. Be sure to completely cover sides. Refrigerate for several hours.

Prepare chocolate sauce by melting the sugar and chocolate in the coffee, simmering for 5 to 6 minutes or until it thickens. Refrigerate until ready to serve.

Spoon about 1/2 cup of the sauce over the top of the cake, creating a marbled effect. Put the remaining sauce in an extra bowl and add a spoonful to each serving.

As this is a very festive looking cake, it is good to use on special occasions. For birthdays and anniversaries, you can put a candle on the top. Bring the cake to the table so the guests can enjoy the unusual effect. When ready to serve, cut off the pyramid top and give to the celebrated guest. Slice the remaining cake and serve.

Serves 8

NUT SLICE WITH MOCHA TOPPING
(Dios Szelet Kave Kremmel)

6 eggs, separated
1-1/4 cups sugar
6-1/2 ounces walnuts, grated
2 tablespoons fine bread crumbs
1 teaspoon cinnamon
1/4 teaspoon ground cloves

Topping
3/4 cup sweet butter
1/2 cup sugar
2 tablespoons instant coffee
1/2 cup strong coffee

Beat egg whites until stiff; add 1/4 cup sugar and beat another 2 to 3 minutes. Set aside.

Cream egg yolks and remaining sugar together; gently fold in egg whites alternately with nuts, bread crumbs, cinnamon, and cloves. Pour into a well-buttered and floured 9x12-inch baking pan and bake in a preheated oven at 350° for 30 minutes.

To make topping cream together butter and sugar. Make a very strong coffee by dissolving the instant coffee in the 1/2 cup coffee, simmering until it evaporates to half the original amount. Cool and gradually add to the butter and sugar mixture, stirring constantly.

When cake is cool, spread mocha cream on top and decorate with a fork dipped in hot water, making long lines across the top. Cut the cake with a sharp knife into small squares or oblongs along the lines.

Serves 6 to 8

CHOCOLATE FROSTING
(Csokolade Bevonas)

1 large bar (8 to 10 ounces) semi-sweet chocolate
2 to 3 tablespoons light, fresh olive oil

Melt chocolate in a double boiler; slowly add oil, stirring until blended. The chocolate should be of a good consistency to pour over a cake. Pour frosting slowly and evenly over cake, letting the frosting spread itself. If necessary, use a spatula to smooth the frosting over the sides, but try not to touch the frosting on top so that it will remain shiny and beautiful.

This is the best and easiest way to get a perfect frosting. Those with whom I have shared this recipe were surprised at the great success.

My double boiler is never empty as I keep the leftover chocolate in it. I just add to it if needed and heat. This is like the old shoemaker's paste bowl that was always in use.

APPLE FRITTERS
(Alma Puffancs)

2 to 3 apples
juice of 1 lemon
1/4 cup rum
1 egg
1/2 cup all-purpose flour
1/2 teaspoon baking powder
1 to 2 teaspoons cream
cinnamon to taste
vegetable oil for deep frying

Peel, core, and slice apples and place in a bowl. Sprinkle with lemon juice and rum, holding some out for garnish.

Mix egg, flour, baking powder, and cream to make a batter. Drain the apples and sprinkle with cinnamon; dip in the batter and deep fry in oil until golden. Drain on absorbent paper.

Warm remaining rum and lemon juice; ignite and pour over the fritters. Serve flaming.

For a lighter fritter, separate egg, mix in yolk, beat white until stiff and fold into batter.

Serves 4 to 6

Cookies, Cakes, Desserts and Candies

RUM CREAM
(Rum Krem)

4 eggs, separated
2 tablespoons all-purpose flour
1/2 cup sugar
1 tablespoon vanilla
1 orange rind, grated
2 cups milk
3 tablespoons rum
1/2 pint whipping cream

Place egg yolks, flour, sugar, vanilla, orange rind, and milk in a double boiler. Beat well until thick. Remove from heat and mix in rum. Fold in well-beaten, stiff egg whites. Divide into individual portions and put in wine glasses. Refrigerate until ready to serve; top with whipped cream.

Serves 6

BUTTER CREAM (BASIC)
(Vaj Krem)

2/3 cup milk
1/2 cup sugar
2 egg yolks
1/2 pound butter, creamed
flavoring (see below)

Put milk in a saucepan with half of the sugar and warm slowly. Remove from heat. Combine egg yolks and remaining sugar until creamy; carefully add hot milk, stirring constantly. Return to heat and stir until mixture thickens. Remove from heat and continue stirring until cool. Add creamed butter, beating all the time; continue beating until thick. Put aside and flavor as desired, using chocolate, instant coffee, orange flavoring, etc. This butter cream will keep in the refrigerator.

Fills and frosts 1 cake

ALMOND DESSERT
(Mandulas Deszert)

1/2 pound Baker's semi-sweet chocolate
2 tablespoons butter
1 3-1/2-ounce package blanched almonds
2 tablespoons sugar

Melt chocolate in a double boiler; stir in butter. Cut blanched almonds into lengthwise pieces several times; in a skillet over low heat toast in sugar until lightly brown. Combine almonds with chocolate. Put small teaspoons of mixture onto waxed paper and let cool and harden.

Keep in boxes in a cool place and put in small cups to serve. This is one of the best candies to offer your guests after dinner.

Serves 8 to 10

CHOCOLATE BOMBS
(Csokolade Bomba)

1/2 pound Baker's semi-sweet chocolate
4 tablespoons butter
2 tablespoons cocoa
1/4 cup sugar
2 egg yolks
toasted filberts or maraschino cherries as needed
chocolate bits used for decorating

Melt chocolate in a double boiler. Add butter, cocoa, sugar, and egg yolks, stirring constantly. Remove from heat and stir until set and cool. Shape into small balls, putting a toasted filbert in the center of each ball. Roll in chocolate bits and serve in little paper cups after meals as one of the best candies.

CHESTNUT RICE
(Gesztenye Pure)

1-1/2 pounds chestnuts
milk as needed
3/4 to 1 cup sugar
1/4 cup water
1 teaspoon vanilla
2 tablespoons rum
1 pint whipping cream for topping

Put chestnuts in a large saucepan and cover with water; boil for 10 minutes. Remove outer and inner peel from chestnuts; take only a few out of the water at a time, as they are easier to peel when warm. Cover peeled chestnuts with milk and simmer until tender and milk is absorbed; press chestnuts through a sieve.

Boil sugar and water to make a thick syrup (don't brown). Immediately add to chestnuts and cool. Add only enough liquid so that the chestnuts can be put through a ricer and still hold their shape. Flavor with vanilla and rum.

Put mixture through a potato ricer, piling high on a nice flat plate. Top with whipped cream. Chill and serve cold as one of the most delicate of fine desserts.

I keep boiled and peeled chestnuts in my freezer all year round. When I need to make a quick dessert, I make chestnut rice which adds a very attractive touch to an elegant meal.

Serves 4 to 6

RICE FRUIT DESSERT
(Gyumolcs Rizs)

1 cup rice
1 cup water
1 cup milk
1 tablespoon vanilla
1/2 cup sugar
1/2 cup blanched, sliced almonds
1 cup cut-up, drained, mixed fruit
   (fresh or canned)
1 pint whipping cream, whipped
liqueur to taste

Simmer rice in water for 20 minutes; add milk and vanilla and simmer until tender, stirring occasionally with a fork so rice won't break. Cool and add sugar, almonds, and fruit; stir in whipped cream. (Save some of the almonds and whipped cream for topping.)

Put in individual wine glasses and refrigerate. When ready to serve, pour liqueur on each serving (Cherry Herring is the best). Top with almonds and whipped cream.

Variation: The cooked rice can be mixed with rum cream (see page 172) instead of whipping cream. Garnish with fruit.

Serves 4 to 6

Cookies, Cakes, Desserts and Candies

MOUSSE AU CHOCOLATE
(Csokolade Krem)

1/2 pound Baker's semi-sweet chocolate
1/2 cup sugar
1/4 cup water
5 eggs, separated
2 teaspoons vanilla
maraschino cherries or slivered almonds for garnish

Melt chocolate in a double boiler. Gradually stir in sugar and water; remove from heat and set aside until lukewarm. Mix egg yolks and vanilla well; add to lukewarm chocolate and fold in well-beaten, stiff egg whites.

Put into wine glasses and chill in the refrigerator for several hours. Top with a cherry or slivered almonds.

Serves 4 to 6

TOASTED NUT MOUSSE WITH CHOCOLATE
(Csokolades Dio Crem)

3 egg yolks
6 tablespoons milk
6 tablespoons sugar
4 squares Baker's semi-sweet chocolate, melted*
1/2 cup toasted, chopped filberts or almonds
1 pint whipping cream, whipped
whole filberts or almonds for topping

Put egg yolks, milk, and sugar in a double boiler and beat until thick. Remove from heat and continue beating until lukewarm. Add chocolate and nuts that have been toasted until lightly brown in a 350° oven. When completely cool, fold in whipped cream (holding some back for topping) and put in wine or champagne glasses. Refrigerate until ready to serve. Top with whipped cream and whole nuts.

This is one of the best flavor combinations, most delicious!

*The easiest way to melt chocolate is to put it on a piece of foil in a warm oven, watching until soft.

Serves 4 to 6

LOW CALORIE FRUIT MOUSSE
(Gyumolcs Hab)

1 cup seasonal fresh ripe fruit, or
   1 cup baked apple pulp
1 egg white
1 cup sugar
1 tablespoon rum

Select soft, ripe fruit and chop into small pieces. (Avoid using raspberries as they have many seeds.) Combine egg white, sugar, and fruit; beat until stiff. Add rum and beat until well mixed.

Serve in individual wine glasses. Refrigerate until ready to serve and top with fresh fruit used in the mousse.

This is a very light and refreshing dessert. In my book, this recipe is titled *haborus crem* or wartime dessert. During the war we didn't have a big choice of rich ingredients for baking. Dairy products, eggs, and sugar were rationed out just to the children.

SNOWBALLS IN VANILLA CREAM
(Madar Tej)

3 eggs, separated
6 tablespoons sugar
2 cups milk
1 tablespoon vanilla
1/4 cup chopped almonds, toasted
   in 1 tablespoon sugar

Beat egg whites until stiff; beat in 1 tablespoon sugar and set aside. Combine milk and vanilla and bring to a boil. Take a large tablespoon of the stiff egg white and put in the simmering milk; repeat a spoonful at a time until the surface of the milk is covered with these snowball-shaped egg whites. Let simmer for 1 to 2 minutes and carefully turn balls over with a slotted spoon. Let simmer in the milk another 1 to 2 minutes and remove to a big glass bowl. Repeat this process until all egg whites have been cooked.

Combine egg yolks with 5 tablespoons sugar; add milk left in the pan. Beat vigorously until sauce thickens. Remove from heat and let cool completely. Pour beside the egg white balls, keeping the white and yellow colors separated. Sprinkle with almonds and refrigerate.

This is believed to be one of the lightest and most delicate of desserts. It is even good for sick people as it is quite nutritious.

Serves 4 to 6

CARAMEL CUSTARD
(Karamel Custard)

Caramel
5 tablespoons sugar
1 tablespoon water

Custard
2/3 cup sugar
1 teaspoon vanilla
4 eggs
1-3/4 cups hot milk

Put 5 tablespoons sugar in a small frying pan; sprinkle with water and brown on low heat. Do not stir but shake pan until golden color. Pour into a 8-inch warm cake pan (not a spring form), turning pan so that the whole bottom and 1-1/2 inches of the sides are covered with the caramel. (The caramel cools and hardens very fast. For this reason, it is important that the cake pan be warm so that the caramel can be spread before hardening.) Cool.

Combine sugar, vanilla, and eggs, stirring slowly with a wooden spoon. Slowly add hot milk, stirring constantly. Pour into cake pan.

Put cake pan in a larger pan of hot water. The water should not come up higher than the middle of the cake pan. Bake in a preheated oven at 350° for 35 to 45 minutes or until done. Test for doneness with a knife; if the knife comes out clean, the custard is done.

Prepare a day ahead and keep in the refrigerator. Turn custard onto a platter with rims. The caramel becomes a very tasty sauce covering the custard.

Serves 4 to 6

BASIC PUFF PASTRY OR FLAKY PASTRY
(Leveles Teszta)

1 pound sweet butter, softened
4 cups sifted flour
1/2 teaspoon salt
1 tablespoon vinegar
2 egg yolks
ice cold water as needed

Put butter and 1 cup flour in a large bowl and work together into a smooth ball. Leave about 1 tablespoon of the flour-butter mixture in the bowl. Form the remaining mixture into a flat square, wrap in waxed paper, and put in the refrigerator.

Add to the bowl 3 cups flour, salt, vinegar, egg yolks, and enough ice water to make a silky-smooth dough. Knead the dough, adding water little by little so that it does not become sticky. Turn onto a floured board, cover, and let stand for 25 to 30 minutes.

Roll out dough into an oblong shape with a floured rolling pin. Place the cold flour and butter mixture in the middle of the rolled out dough and fold sides over tightly, bringing each into the center; the butter should be surrounded evenly by the dough. Roll out with a floured rolling pin into an oblong a little over 1 inch thick. Be careful that the dough does not break or the butter come out, yet avoid adding too much additional flour which changes the proportions.

Reroll dough, fold as before, put in waxed paper and cool for 30 minutes in the refrigerator. Repeat entire process of rolling, folding and refrigerating two more times.

This dough is the most simple and makes miracles if handled correctly. It is most important to keep the dough cool, working in a cool place and not handling the dough too much with your warm hands. The dough should be firm—not too hard or too soft. After you have had some experience handling the dough, it will become easier.

This dough can be prepared ahead and kept in the refrigerator for 2 weeks; just take out as much as needed. One can make a great variety of desserts, cocktails, and hors d'oeuvre from the dough.

Roll dough according to the desired size and thickness. For cocktails, make smaller squares filled with ham or mushroom or just sprinkle with grated cheese and paprika; for desserts, make bigger squares with cheese filling or two rounds put together with raspberry jam or whipped cream, dusting the top generously with powdered sugar or icing, after cooking.

Bake in preheated 450° oven 10 minutes; reduce heat and cook until golden.

Serves 6 to 8

FLAKY CHEESE SQUARES
(Leveles Turos Taska)

2 eggs, separated
1/2 cup sugar
1 tablespoon butter
1 teaspoon vanilla
1 teaspoon lemon juice
1 tablespoon cream of wheat
1 pound baker's cheese
1 teaspoon grated lemon rind
1/2 cup raisins
1 recipe puff pastry dough, preceding
1 egg, beaten

Beat egg whites until stiff. Cream together egg yolks, sugar, butter, vanilla, lemon juice, cream of wheat, and baker's cheese. Fold in egg whites, lemon rind, and raisins.

Put a teaspoon of this mixture on the middle of a 3-inch square of dough. Put a little beaten egg on the corner of the square for sealing; fold dough over the filling and secure so that it won't open while baking.

Brush squares with the beaten egg. Bake in preheated 450° oven 10 minutes; reduce to 350° and cook until golden.

Serves 6

Beverages

I have tried to introduce the habits and customs of my old country throughout this book, but they are just tiny mosaics of the whole. Even though Hungary is a small country due to the wars and revolutions, the people there are great and blessed with big talents and ambitions. Their art, music, and high culture are well known throughout the world.

As a famous Hungarian poet says:

"Ki Duna vizet itta
Vagyik annak szive vissza."

"Who once tasted the water of Danube
Longs in her heart to return to it."

This is true even though I have sad memories, too. But I am thankful and happy now where my family and I found a new home, new friends, and a wonderful place to live.

This chapter has made me very nostalgic, as it brings back many of my memories: the vineyard, the country, the gorgeous scenery with hills and meadows full of grapevines and flowers, vintage and harvest songs and melodies.

Beverages

WINES
(Borok)

Hungary is well known as one of the largest winegrowing countries. The hills and mountains, as well as the climate and soil, contribute to the production of a great variety of fine wines.

Somehow the wine is perfect in harmony with sugar, alcohol, and acid, and through its very agreeable taste is a pleasant beverage for everybody.

Tokay Aszu is a well-known, sweet-flavored wine. The grapes are picked very late in the fall. To increase the sweetness, more raisin-type grapes are added to the wine. These grapes are picked almost in the early winter and used in the proportion of two to five pails, *puttonyos,* per barrel, according to desired sweetness.

If one is a winegrower, one also becomes quite a meteorologist. If it is cold in the early spring, low fires are made so that the smoke will save the blossoms from the frost. In the summer there is danger from a moth-type caterpillar. Through the night torches are burned above big basins of water and in the morning the basins are full of these insects. The leaves are also sprayed with chemicals in the summer to prevent the worst disease—the pernospora. The leaves are necessary to protect the grapes from the biggest enemy—hail. I can remember once we were away one week from the vintage and hail ruined our entire harvest.

Our people knew from the clouds which way the wind was blowing and from the coloring of the sky what type of weather to expect.

The wine in Badacsony is famous due to the special soil. The consistency of the earth and the shapes of the mountains show that they are volcanic in origin.

Badacsony Keknyelu (blue neck) grapes make the finest, very dry white wine. The grey and green riesling is the full-bodied, golden-colored, dry wine. The Badacsony Szurkebarat (grey monk) is the heaviest white wine. The Auvergnas Gris is the most flavorful muscatel with the best bouquet and a light golden color. The Csasla grapes make a sweet wine but are used mostly as grapes for the table. Some are hung and saved until spring.

The burgundy is light, smooth, and dry with no acid aftertaste. If we wanted the full body and red color, we soaked the juice or "must" of the grapes overnight with the stems and skins.

I loved the smell of the wine cellar and our huge barrels; they were kept extremely clean and shiny outside and were always filled up to the rim to maintain the golden color and the perfect taste of the wine.

Inside the barrels a special wine tartar forms which helps to ripen the wine. If there is too much of it, however, it is bad for the wine. When this happened, young people were sent inside the barrels with hammers to remove the excess tartar.

Well-chosen wines can add a great enjoyment to almost every meal. Sometimes they are mixed with sparkling water which makes the most refreshing of drinks.

White wine should be served chilled—not too long because it takes away from the flavor. Red wines are served at a cool room temperature. It is advisable to open the wine a half hour before serving which brings the flavor out better. Wine bottles should be stored on their sides in a cool, dark place. When serving, pour carefully to eliminate the sediment from the bottom.

When the State took away our vineyards, I—the old winemaker—tried to ferment my own wine at home from all kinds of fruit. The best result I had was from red currant—delicious.

The appropriate use of wines served correctly will add a special touch to even the most simple meals: with fish, light meat, and poultry serve chilled, dry white wine; with dark meat serve slightly chilled red wine; with desserts serve chilled, sweet wine; after meals serve cognac or liqueur at room temperature.

BRANDYS
(Palinkak)

The Hungarian apricot brandy *barack palinka* is known over the whole world and is distilled from this exquisitely flavored fruit. Other hard liqueurs are made from all kinds of fruits and nuts.

In the vineyard, we preserved the pressed, almost dry stems and skins in huge, well-covered trenches until fermented. The grape skins and the residue from the barrels are dried and distilled separately by a special procedure. Both make a strong, raw brandy. In the winter it is customary for hard-working laborers to start their morning out with a shot of this heart-warming drink.

MULLED WINE
(Forralt Bor)

It is an old belief in Hungary that mulled wine is the best remedy for a cold or the flu. Put a decanter full of hot, mulled wine at your bedside, put a hat on the other end of your bed, and drink the wine until you see two hats. Then stop drinking and cover yourself with a heavy blanket. You will have a good night's sleep and wake up healthy. This cure is called *kalap kura,* or the hat cure.

Mulled wine can be made from white or red wine, sugar to taste, some whole cinnamon and clove, and orange or lemon rind—serve very hot. This is a popular winter drink to serve when people come in from the cold.

CHAMPAGNE
(Pezsgo)

Champagne is always appropriate served well chilled. One year our harvest didn't turn out the usual high-alcohol percentage of our wines. We sold it to a champagne factory and as a present we received cases full of champagne made from our own wine. This was great fun to have.

Champagne is festive and makes every meal a celebration. It has traditionally been used for toasts on special occasions. On New Year's Eve, *Sylvester,* a glass of champagne and a kiss are indispensable.

Beverages

VERMOUTH

The "happy hour" of drinks and cocktails is not known in Hungary. The only aperitif served before meals is a glass of fine vermouth. The bitter taste of the vermouth is believed to stimulate and improve the appetite. After dinner the finest French cognacs or sweet liqueurs are served.

ESPRESSO COFFEE
(Expresso Kave)

Hungary serves espresso coffee perhaps even more than Italy. We have all kinds of special coffee makers which steam the finely ground coffee. Through the big pressure one gets very little liquid out but each drop is full of caffeine. The coffee is served in demitasse cups at any time of the day to get fresh energy for hard work. It is always freshly roasted and ground just before making. In very cold weather, a little rum is sometimes added to each cup of coffee.

TURKISH COFFEE
(Torok Kave)

For each serving, put 2 teaspoons coffee, that has been ground well into a powder, and 1 teaspoon sugar in a small pot. Pour 1/2 cup cold water over and bring to a boil over low heat. Remove from heat until boiling stops; return to heat and bring to a second boil; repeat this procedure 3 times in all. Add a teaspoon of cold water to the pot and let stand 2 to 3 minutes. This will settle the grounds. Pour and serve.

The real coffee connoisseur drinks it without sugar, or takes a lump of sugar in his mouth while drinking. The coffee is cooked with a little sugar to bring out and preserve the aroma.

Index

Index

Index

Biographical Data

CHARLOTTE SLOVAK BIRO

Born in Budapest in 1904, Charlotte Slovak studied music and languages. Both as a girl and after her marriage to banker Zoltan Biro her summers were spent at the family vineyards in Badacsony, where her interest and knowledge of food and wine were developed.

In 1949 the Biro family attempted to escape Communist-dominated Hungary. Their daughters succeeded in getting through to Vienna and subsequently to America, but Charlotte Biro and her husband were arrested and imprisoned. The only possessions she had with her were the family cookbooks, containing three generations of handwritten recipes. Because of these she was put to work in the prison kitchen.

In 1957 Mrs. Biro legally left Hungary and came to the United States, bringing her precious cookbooks with her. It is these recipes, shown below, translated and adapted to American measurements and ingredients, that comprise the nucleus of this book.

Charlotte Biro presently lives in San Francisco where she has taught cooking classes.

LINDA ROBERTSON

Prior to Flavors of Hungary, Linda Robertson illustrated two other 101 Productions cookbooks: Flavors of India and Herb Cookery, which received an Award of Merit for design in the Western Art Directors Club Eighth Annual Exhibition of Communicating Arts. She has a degree in fine arts from Washington University in St. Louis and presently works in San Francisco as a free-lance graphic designer and artist.